Lone Pine Publishing

Annuals *for* Illinois

William Aldrich
Don Williamson

The Publisher: Lone Pine Publishing

10145 – 81 Avenue   1808 – B Street NW, Suite 140
Edmonton, AB, Canada T6E 1W9   Auburn, WA, USA 98001

Website: www.lonepinepublishing.com

National Library of Canada Cataloguing in Publication Data

Aldrich, William, 1948–
   Annuals of Illinois / William Aldrich.

Includes index.
   ISBN 1-55105-380-2

   1. Annuals (Plants)—Illinois. I. Williamson, Don, 1962– II. Title.
SB422.A42 2004   635.9'312'09773   C2003-910882-1

Editorial Director: Nancy Foulds
Project Editor: Dawn Loewen
Illustrations Coordinator: Carol Woo
Researcher: Alison Beck
Photo Editor: Don Williamson
Production Manager: Gene Longson
Book Design & Layout: Heather Markham
Production Support: Jeff Fedorkiw, Lynett McKell, Elliot Engley
Cover Design: Gerry Dotto
Scanning, Separations & Film: Elite Lithographers Co.

All photos by **Tim Matheson** or **Tamara Eder** except **All-America Selections** 13a, 35b, 85a,
89b, 216b, 217b, 243a, 262a, 269a, 271b; **Ball Horticultural Co.** 93b; **Doris Baucom** 213b;
David Cavagnaro 92, 96, 97a&b, 99a, 125b, 222; **Elliot Engley** 25b, 26, 27a&b, 28a&b&c;
EuroAmerican 75b, 111a, 134, 135a, 136a, 137a&b, 183a, 212, 213a, 283a; **Jennifer Fafard**
157a; **Derek Fell** 50, 51a&b, 52a&b, 53b, 78b, 80a, 98a, 126b, 127a&b, 143a, 195a, 203a,
223a&b, 231a&b, 261a, 262b; **Anne Gordon** 59a, 210; **Joan de Grey** 16a, 53a, 93a, 98b, 99b,
171a; **Saxon Holt** 67b; **Horticolor** 282a; **Horticultural Photography: Arthur N. Orans** 59b;
Debra Knapke 65b, 66b, 67a, 91a&b, 159a&b, 170, 171b, 211b; **Colin Laroque** 10; **Janet
Loughrey** 211a; **Kim O'Leary** 13b, 29a, 31a, 58, 65a, 78a, 90, 118a, 131a&b, 132, 135b, 139a,
141a, 163a&b, 176, 177, 193b, 209a, 233a, 261b, 263b, 265a; **Allison Penko** 108b; **Proven
Winners** 81a; **Robert Ritchie** 42b, 44b, 46b; **Aleksandra Szywala** 81b, 202, 203b; **Peter
Thompstone** 63a&b, 103b, 122, 123a, 141b, 173a, 174a&b, 219a, 247b

Cover photos: by Tim Matheson, fuchsia, sunflower, dahlia, gazania; by Tamara Eder,
Mexican sunflower

Map: frost-date data from National Oceanic and Atmospheric Administration National
Climatic Data Center, Asheville, North Carolina

We acknowledge the financial support of the Government of Canada through the Book Publishing Industry Development Program (BPIDP) for our publishing activities.

PC: *P1*

CONTENTS

ACKNOWLEDGMENTS

We gratefully acknowledge all who were involved in this project, as well as the many gorgeous public and private gardens that provided the setting for photographs in this book. Special thanks are extended to the following individuals and organizations: Barbara and Douglas Bloom, Thea and Don Bloomquist, Heidi Clausen, Robert Ritchie, Peter Thompstone, Agriculture Canada Central Experimental Farm, Bordine Nursery, Casa Loma Gardens, Chicago Botanic Garden, Cranbrook Gardens, Cranbrook Garden Auxiliary, Cullen Gardens, Edwards Gardens, Inniswood Metro Gardens, Montreal Botanic Garden, Morton Arboretum, Niagara Parks Botanical Gardens and Royal Botanical Gardens.

Learning about gardening is a lifelong passion that has to begin somewhere. Thanks to Anna Lee Trapani for getting me started and providing her kindred spirit through the years. Josh Schneider, former owner of Mourning Dove Farms in Mahomet and now national spokesman for the Proven Winners brand of annuals, provided invaluable insight in keeping all the series and cultivars straight. Liz Omura of Cantigny Gardens in Wheaton likewise added counsel and advice. Cantigny's Idea Garden is now one of the state's more innovative gardens and can trace its beginnings to a humble plot known as The Cook's Garden, where I received my horticultural apprenticeship.—*William Aldrich*

I thank The Creator.—*Don Williamson*

THE FLOWERS AT A GLANCE

A PICTORIAL GUIDE IN ALPHABETICAL ORDER, BY COMMON NAME

African Daisy
p. 50

Ageratum
p. 54

Agrostemma
p. 58

Amaranth
p. 60

Angel's Trumpet
p. 64

Angel Wings
p. 68

Baby's Breath
p. 70

Bachelor's Buttons
p. 72

Bacopa
p. 74

Begonia
p. 76

Bidens
p. 82

Black-eyed Susan
p. 84

Black-eyed Susan Vine
p. 86

Blanket Flower
p. 88

Blood Flower
p. 90

Blue Throatwort
p. 92

Browallia
p. 94

Caladium
p. 96

Calibrachoa
p. 102

Canterbury Bells
p. 104

Cockscomb
p. 106

Calendula
p. 100

Coleus
p. 110

Coreopsis
p. 114

Creeping Zinnia
p. 120

Cup Flower
p. 122

Cuphea
p. 124

Cosmos
p. 116

Dahlberg Daisy
p. 128

Dahlia
p. 130

Diascia
p. 134

Fan Flower
p. 140

Flowering Maple
p. 142

Flowering Tobacco
p. 146

Dusty Miller
p. 138

Four O'Clock Flower
p. 150

Geranium
p. 158

Globe Amaranth
p. 162

Fuchsia
p. 152

Gazania
p. 156

Hollyhock
p. 168

Hyacinth Bean
p. 170

Impatiens
p. 172

Heliotrope
p. 164

Lantana
p. 176

Larkspur
p. 178

Licorice Plant
p. 182

Lobelia
p. 184

Lavatera
p. 180

Love-in-a-Mist
p. 186

Marigold
p. 188

Mexican Sunflower
p. 192

Mignonette
p. 194

Monkey Flower
p. 196

Morning Glory
p. 198

Nasturtium
p. 204

Nemesia
p. 208

Musk Mallow
p. 202

Passion Flower
p. 210

Persian Shield
p. 212

Petunia
p. 214

Phlox
p. 218

Pincushion Flower
p. 220

Polka Dot Plant
p. 222

Poppy
p. 224

Portulaca
p. 228

Rose-of-Heaven
p. 230

Salvia
p. 232

Snapdragon
p. 236

Spider Flower
p. 240

Statice
p. 244

Strawflower
p. 248

Stock
p. 246

Sunflower
p. 250

Swan River Daisy
p. 254

Sweet Alyssum
p. 256

Sweet Pea
p. 258

Sweet William
p. 260

Verbena
p. 264

Vinca
p. 268

Viola
p. 270

Wishbone Flower
p. 274

Xeranthemum
p. 276

Zinnia
p. 278

INTRODUCTION

Somewhere out in the greenhouse is a colorfully painted terra cotta pot that came home from school once upon a childhood. Originally, there must have been a marigold in that pot, perhaps with a single sunny bloom. That marigold once grew in a flat with many others until the day that youthful hands tucked it into the pot. Every spring in local garden centers, we can find similar flats brimming with bright colors, begging to be taken home and planted in our pots and garden beds. They will amaze us over the course of the next several months, but we replace them the following year with more of the same or with the newest passing fancy. These plants have become known as annuals.

True annuals are plants that complete their full life cycle in one growing season. Within one year they germinate, mature, bloom, set seed and die. Some plants grown as annuals are actually tender perennials or even shrubs; these plants cannot survive our winters but grow quickly enough to be planted anew each year.

Annuals are sometimes referred to as bedding plants because they are used to fill in garden beds and provide color. Most annuals are started indoors and then transplanted into the garden after the last spring frost, but some can be sown directly in the garden.

The information in this book covers all areas of Illinois. Although the state is geographically diverse, growing conditions for annuals are relatively similar in all regions. Still, you should be aware of the particular conditions in your area and garden. Keeping a journal or diary of climate conditions is a useful aid to garden planning.

Annuals make great plant choices for Illinois because most are adaptable to our variable summers. Given sufficient moisture, they are generally not bothered by 90° F temperatures or by a sudden cool snap. Like all plants, annuals prefer optimal growing conditions, but most seem to cope with the unpredictable growing conditions of our state.

Illinois generally receives enough moisture during the growing season to support a wide range of plants. Much of the state receives 30–40" of precipitation per year, with some downstate counties averaging as much as 45" per year. But if you assign an inch of water per week as the optimal amount, you know that the diligent gardener will need to provide some supplemental moisture with the watering can.

The length of the growing season determines how long annuals last in the garden. In Illinois, the last killing frost can occur at any time between early April and early May (see map). Lake Michigan affects areas within a few miles of its shore by moderating late cold snaps and early fall chills, making the growing season a couple of weeks longer than in inland areas. Latitude also influences length of growing season. On average, in some northern counties, there may be fewer than 160 frost-free days each year versus more than 200 in a few southerly counties. All Illinois gardeners can expect a frost-free period of at least five months, plenty of time for annuals to mature and fill the garden with color.

Soil temperature is another determining factor in spring planting decisions. Many annual seeds need warm soil before they will germinate. Growth of some plants may be slowed if they are planted into cool soil. The plant entries in this book indicate minimum soil temperatures for seeding or planting out as appropriate.

Gardeners are famous for rushing the season, so garden centers know they can sell more annuals if they are well stocked at an earlier date than is safe for planting. Then, when the late last frost rolls through, the early-bird gardener has to return to purchase a second round of plants. This book will help you determine which annuals are worth the early gamble and which annuals require more patience.

Annuals are popular because they produce abundant flowers in a wide variety of colors over a long period of time. Many annuals bloom continuously from spring through early fall. Beyond this basic appeal, gardeners constantly find new ways to include annuals in their gardens, using them to accent areas in an established border, featuring them as the main attraction in a new garden or combining them with trees, shrubs, perennials and even vegetables. Many annuals are adapted to a variety of growing conditions, from hot, dry sun to cool, damp shade. They are fun for beginners and experienced gardeners alike, and because annuals are temporary and inexpensive, they can be easily replaced.

Average Last-Frost Date

LEGEND
- May 5
- Apr 28
- Apr 21
- Apr 14
- Apr 7
- Mar 31

Some annuals are widely grown every year. Some of the most popular, easy-to-grow and reliable annuals include geraniums, petunias, impatiens, marigolds and zinnias. In recent years, gardeners have also developed an interest in unusual annuals, such as caladium, cuphea and wishbone flower.

The selection of annuals increases every year. Even for the old favorites, there are always newly developed cultivars to try, often with an expanded color range or increased disease resistance. Some beautiful plants that have been overlooked in the past because they bloom later in summer are now in wider use. New species have been introduced from other parts of the world. The use of heritage varieties has been revived because many gardeners are concerned with overhybridization, have an interest in organic gardening or appreciate that many older varieties have more fragrance.

AAS winner 'Corona Cherry Magic' sweet william

When new varieties are introduced, some may experience a short period of popularity but are soon forgotten. Others are entered in trials that compare each variety to a similar one already on the market. These trials are conducted across the United States and Canada. The varieties judged superior in many regions are certified as All-America Selections. These varieties should perform well in most gardens. Look for the distinctive 'All-America Selections Winner' symbol in seed catalogs and on plant tags at garden centers and nurseries. See also the AAS website: <http://www.all-americaselections.org/>.

Dahlia, marigold & coreopsis

ANNUAL GARDENS

Annuals are often combined with woody plants and herbaceous perennials. Where trees and shrubs form the permanent structure or the 'bones' of the garden, and perennials and groundcovers occupy the spaces between them, annuals add bold patterns and bright splashes of color. Using a variety of annuals in the garden can ensure continuous color, bridging the blooming gaps of other plants.

Annuals are also perfect for filling in bare spaces around small or leggy shrubs or between perennials that sprout late in the season. Annual vines can create a temporary screen to hide an undesirable view or an unattractive part of the garden, such as a compost pile, old fence or shed. Include annuals anywhere that you would like some variety and an extra splash of color—in pots staggered up porch steps or on a deck, in windowsill planters or in hanging baskets. Even well-established gardens are brightened by the addition of annual flowers.

The short life of annuals allows gardeners a large degree of flexibility and freedom when they plan a garden. Annuals give us the opportunity to make the same garden look different each year. Even something as simple as a planting of impatiens under a tree can be different each year with different varieties and color combinations.

There are many styles of gardens, and annuals can be used in any of them. A well-kept, symmetrical, formal garden can be enhanced by adding only a few types of annuals or by choosing annuals that all have the same flower color. Add a dash of the informal to the same garden by including many different species and colors of annuals to break up formal tree and shrub plantings.

An informal, cottage-style garden can become a riot of plants and colors. The same garden will look less disorganized and even soothing if you use several species that bloom in cool shades of blue and purple. You can create whatever style garden you desire by cleverly mixing annuals.

When planning your garden, consult as many sources as you can. Look through gardening books and ask friends and gardening experts for advice. Notice what you like or dislike about various gardens, and make a list of the plants you would like to include in your garden.

Finding the right annuals for your garden will require experimentation, creativity and planning. Most people make the color, size and shape of the blossoms their prime considerations when choosing annuals. Other attributes to consider are the size and shape of the whole plant and its leaves. Including a variety of flower and plant sizes, shapes and colors will make your garden more interesting. Consult the Quick Reference Chart on pp. 284–89 to help you plan.

Annuals of different colors have different effects on our senses. The cool colors—purple, blue and green—are soothing, so annuals such as lobelia, ageratum and browallia can make a small garden appear larger. The warm colors—red, orange, yellow—are more stimulating, so annuals such as scarlet salvia, calendula and Mexican sunflower appear to fill larger spaces. Warm colors can make even the largest, most imposing garden welcoming.

If you have time to enjoy your garden only in the evenings, consider pale colors. White and yellow show up well at dusk and even at night. Some plants

Sweet potato vine

have flowers that open only in the evenings, often with a fragrance that further enhances the evening garden. Moonflower is a twining plant with large, white, fragrant flowers that open when the sun sets.

Don't forget to consider foliage in your plans for annuals. Some annuals are grown solely for their interesting or colorful foliage and can look particularly attractive in mixed hanging baskets and planters. Leaves can be any shade of green or multiple shades. They may be covered in a soft white down and appear silvery, or they can be so dark that they appear almost black. Some foliage is patterned or has veins that contrast with the main color of the leaves. Some foliage plants, such as coleus, are so striking they can be used on their own as specimens; others, such as sweet potato vine, provide an interesting backdrop against brightly colored flowers.

ANNUALS WITH INTERESTING FOLIAGE

- Amaranth 'Illumination'
- Caladium
- Coleus
- Nasturtium
- Polka dot plant
- Rex begonia
- Sweet potato vine
- Zonal geranium

Texture is another element to consider when planning a garden. Both flowers and foliage have a visual texture. Large leaves appear coarse, making a garden seem smaller and more shaded. Coarse-textured flowers look bold and dramatic and can be seen from a distance. Small leaves appear fine, creating a sense of increased space and light. Fine-textured flowers look soothing and even a little mysterious. Some annuals have flowers and foliage with contrasting textures. Using a variety of textures helps make a garden interesting and appealing.

The great thing about using annuals to achieve these various effects is that you can easily change your mind the very next time you plant.

COARSE-TEXTURED ANNUALS

- Amaranth
- Angel's trumpet
- Flowering tobacco
- Hollyhock
- Opium poppy
- Sunflower
- Sweet potato vine
- Zinnia

FINE-TEXTURED ANNUALS

- Baby's breath
- Bacopa
- Cup flower
- Larkspur
- Lobelia
- Love-in-a-mist
- Swan River daisy
- Sweet alyssum

Opium poppy (above), lobelia (below)

Caladium

Getting Started

Before you rush to the garden center to buy your annuals, consider the growing conditions in your garden. These conditions will influence not only the types of plants that you select, but also the locations in which you plant them. For hot, dry areas or for low-lying, damp sections of the garden, select plants that prefer those conditions. The plants will be healthier and less susceptible to problems if grown in optimum conditions. Because it is difficult to significantly modify your garden's existing conditions, match the plants to the garden instead.

Criteria to consider when selecting plants include light levels; soil texture, pH and fertility; the amount of exposure in your garden; and the plants' frost tolerance. Sketching your garden may help you visualize the various conditions. Your sketch should include shaded areas, low-lying or wet areas and exposed or windy sections. Then consult the Quick Reference Chart on pp. 284–89 and the individual plant entries to find annuals suited to those conditions. Experimenting with annuals will in turn help you learn about the conditions of your garden. If you make a mistake, the plants are easy and relatively inexpensive to replace.

Understanding your garden's growing conditions will help you learn to recognize which plants will perform best, and it can also prevent you from making costly mistakes in your planting decisions.

Light

Four levels of light may be present in a garden: full sun, partial shade, light shade and full shade. Available light is affected by buildings, trees, fences and the position of the sun at different

or all of the day, but some sunlight does filter through to ground level. An example of a light-shade location is the ground under a small-leaved tree such as a birch. **Full shade** locations, such as the north side of a house, receive no direct sunlight.

Sun-loving plants may become tall and straggly and flower poorly in too much shade. Shade-loving plants may get scorched leaves or even wilt and die if they get too much sun. Many plants tolerate a range of light conditions.

times of the day and year. Knowing what light is available in your garden will help you determine where to place each plant.

Plants in **full sun** locations, such as along south-facing walls or other southern exposures, receive direct sun for at least six hours a day. Locations classified as **partial shade,** such as east- or west-facing walls, receive direct morning or late-afternoon sun and then shade for the rest of the day. **Light shade** locations receive shade for most

Portulaca (above), browallia (below)

ANNUALS FOR FULL SUN

African daisy
Amaranth
Blanket flower
Cosmos
Geranium
Marigold
Portulaca
Spider flower
Statice

ANNUALS FOR PARTIAL SHADE

Bacopa
Begonia
Browallia
Canterbury bells
Coleus
Impatiens
Viola

ANNUALS FOR SUN OR SHADE

Black-eyed Susan
Black-eyed Susan vine
Blue throatwort
Cup flower
Flowering tobacco
Lobelia
Morning glory
Passion flower
Vinca

Soil

Soil quality is an extremely important element of a healthy garden. Plant roots rely on the air, water and nutrients that are held within soil. Plants also depend on soil to hold them upright. In turn, the soil benefits from plant roots breaking down large clods. Plants prevent soil erosion by binding together small particles and reducing the amount of exposed surface. When plants die and break down, they add organic nutrients to soil and feed beneficial microorganisms.

Soil is made up of particles of different sizes. Sand particles are the largest—water drains quickly from sandy soil and nutrients tend to get washed away. Sandy soil does not compact very easily because the large particles leave air pockets between them. Clay particles, which are the smallest, can be seen only through a microscope. Clay holds the most nutrients, but it also compacts easily and has little air space. Clay is slow to absorb water and equally slow to let it drain. Most soils are loams, composed of a combination of different particle sizes.

The pH level of soil—the indicator of its acidity or alkalinity—influences the availability of nutrients. Most plants thrive in soil with a pH between 5.5 and 7.5. Much of the Chicago area has a relatively high (alkaline) pH, to the point of needing acidic amendments to help plants grow to their optimum. Each garden is different and should be tested, not only for pH but also for nutrient levels. Simple test kits can be purchased at most garden centers. There are also soil-testing labs that can fully analyze the pH and levels of various nutrients in your soil.

Black-eyed Susan

The addition of elemental sulfur will lower soil pH, but it takes a long time for the effects to become permanent. For quick results, use aluminum sulfate or ammonium sulfate. Acidity can be corrected by adding horticultural lime or wood ash, which is extremely alkaline. Do not use wood ash from such sources as treated lumber or pallets.

If you wish to grow plants that prefer a pH different from that in your garden soil, consider growing them in planters or raised beds where it is easier to control and alter the soil's pH. Always check the pH and other soil properties before you import any soil, purchased or otherwise, into your garden.

Water drainage is affected by soil type and terrain in your garden. Plants that prefer well-drained soil and do not require a large amount of moisture grow well on a sloping hillside with

ANNUALS FOR MOIST SOIL

Ageratum
Angel's trumpet
Bacopa
Black-eyed Susan vine
Monkey flower
Persian shield
Spider flower
Viola
Wishbone flower

ANNUALS FOR DRY SOIL

Baby's breath
Blanket flower
Blood flower
Coreopsis
Cosmos
Marigold
Mexican sunflower
Portulaca
Zinnia

rocky soil. Water retention in these areas can be improved through the addition of organic matter. Plants that thrive on a consistent water supply or boggy conditions are ideal for low-lying areas that retain water for longer periods or hardly drain at all, such as at the base of a slope. In extremely wet areas, you can improve drainage by adding gravel and installing drainage tile. Raised beds can also be used.

Monkey flower (above), zinnia (below)

Exposure

Your garden is exposed to wind, heat, cold and rain, and some plants are better adapted than others to withstand the potential damage of these forces. Buildings, walls, fences, hills, hedges, trees and even tall perennials influence and often reduce exposure.

Wind and heat are the most likely elements to cause damage to annuals. The sun can be very intense, and heat can rise quickly on a sunny afternoon. Plant annuals that tolerate or even thrive in hot weather in the hot spots in your garden.

Too much rain can damage annuals, as can overwatering. Early in the season, seeds or seedlings can be washed away in heavy rain. A light mulch or grow cover will help prevent this problem. Established annuals (or their flowers) can be destroyed by heavy rain. Most annuals will recover, but some, such as petunias, are slow to do so. For exposed sites, choose plants or varieties that are quick to recover from rain damage. Many of the small-flowered petunia varieties now available recover well from the effects of heavy rain.

Hanging moss-lined baskets are particularly exposed to wind and heat. Water can evaporate from all sides of a moss basket, and in hot or windy locations, moisture can be depleted very quickly. Hanging baskets look wonderful, but watch for wilting and water regularly to keep them looking great. These baskets will hold up better in adverse conditions if you soak the moss or other liner in a wetting agent (see p. 34) and add some of the wetting agent to the water when first watering.

Frost Tolerance

When planting annuals, consider their ability to tolerate an unexpected frost. Last-frost and first-frost dates vary greatly from year to year and region to region in North America. They can also vary considerably within each general region. The map on p. 12 gives a general idea of when you can expect the last frost in your region; consult your local garden center for more specific information.

Annuals are grouped into three categories based on how tolerant they are of cold weather: hardy, half-hardy or tender. The Quick Reference Chart on pp. 284–89 indicates the hardiness of the annuals discussed in this book.

Hardy annuals tolerate low temperatures and even frost. They can be planted in the garden early and may continue to flower long into fall or even winter. Many hardy annuals are sown directly in the garden before the last-frost date.

Half-hardy annuals can tolerate a light frost but will be killed by a heavy one. These annuals can be planted out around the last-frost date and will generally benefit from being started early from seed indoors.

Tender annuals have no frost tolerance at all and might suffer if the temperatures drop to even a few degrees above freezing. These plants are often started early indoors and not planted in the garden until the last-frost date has passed and the ground has had a chance to warm up. These annuals often have the advantage of tolerating hot summer temperatures.

Protecting plants from frost is relatively simple. Cover them overnight with sheets, towels, burlap, row covers or even cardboard boxes. Refrain from using plastic because it doesn't retain heat and therefore won't provide your plants with any insulation.

Marigolds & impatiens are frost tender.

PREPARING THE GARDEN

Properly preparing your flowerbeds before seeding or transplanting saves you time and effort over the summer and prevents many gardening problems. To give your annuals a good start, begin with as few weeds as possible and with a well-prepared soil enriched with organic matter.

Every spring, loosen the soil with a garden fork and remove the weeds. Avoid working the soil when it is very wet or very dry, or you may damage the soil structure by breaking down the pockets that hold air and water. Work organic matter into the soil with a spade or power tiller. For containers, use potting mix. Regular garden soil loses its structure in pots, quickly compacting into a solid mass that drains poorly.

Organic matter is a very important component of soil. It increases the water-holding and nutrient-holding capacity of sandy soil and binds together the large particles. Organic matter increases a clay soil's ability to absorb and drain water by opening up spaces between the tiny particles. Common organic additives for your soil include grass clippings, shredded leaves, peat moss, chopped straw, well-rotted manure, alfalfa pellets and compost. Alfalfa pellets supply a range of nutrients, including trace elements, as well as a plant growth hormone.

Composting

Most organic matter you add to your garden will be of greater benefit if it has been composted first. Composted organic matter adds nutrients and improves soil structure. Decaying organic matter releases acids and can help lower the pH in alkaline soils. If your soil is acidic and has lots of organic matter, amendments and time are needed to raise the pH.

In forests or meadows, compost is created when leaves, plant bits and other debris are broken down on the soil surface. This process will also take place in your garden beds if you work fresh organic matter into the soil. However, microorganisms that break down organic matter use the same nutrients as your plants. The tougher the organic matter, the more nutrients in the soil will be used breaking it down. As a result, your plants will be robbed of vital nutrients, particularly nitrogen. Also, fresh organic matter and garden debris can encourage or introduce pests and diseases in your garden.

A compost pile or bin creates a controlled environment where organic matter can be fully broken down. Good composting methods also reduce the possibility of spreading pests and diseases. Compost can be made in a pile, in a wooden box or in a purchased compost bin. Two methods can be used; neither is complicated, but the first requires more effort.

The 'active' or hot composting method requires you to turn the pile every week or so during the growing season. Frequent turning creates compost faster, but because the compost generates a lot of heat, some beneficial microorganisms that help fight diseases are killed. If you prefer the active approach to composting, look in our *Perennials for Illinois*, or in any of several good books on composting. The University of Illinois Extension has several publications, or check their website: <http://www.urbanext.uiuc.edu/compost/process.html>.

For many gardeners, the easier method, 'passive' or cold composting, is the more practical approach. Making a passive compost pile involves simply dumping yard waste into a pile. This material may include weeds pulled from the garden, pruned branches cut into small pieces, leftover grass clippings, fall leaves, and fruit and vegetable scraps. Never compost meat scraps. Avoid putting weed seeds and diseased or pest-ridden plants into your compost pile, or you risk spreading problems throughout your garden.

Grass clippings should be left on the lawn for the most part, but you can collect them every couple of weeks to add to the pile. Similarly, some fallen leaves should be chopped up with a mulching mower and left on the lawn; some can be collected, shredded and used as mulch under shrubs and on flowerbeds; and the remainder can be composted. Many gardeners collect leaves from neighbors, store them in plastic bags and add them to their compost pile over the following year.

After a season or two, the passive pile will have a layer of pure black gold at the bottom that looks much like the leaf mold found in the woods. Your finished compost can be accessed by moving the top of the pile aside. Spread the finished compost on the surface of the garden bed, or, if compost is in short supply, just add a trowelful to each planting hole.

Many municipalities now recycle yard wastes into compost that is made available to residents. Contact your city hall to see if this valuable resource is available to you. Compost can also be purchased from most garden centers.

If you have limited space, consider worm composting. The process is simple. Get a plastic container and punch in drainage and air holes. Place a layer of shredded newspaper (avoid glossy newsprint) into the container and moisten it so it is about as wet as a wrung-out sponge. Add red worms, which are available at any bait shop, along with your kitchen scraps (minus any meat products). The worms will break down the material, and you can have black, nutrient-rich worm castings in as few as six weeks.

Selecting Annuals

Many gardeners consider the trip to the local garden center to choose their annuals an important rite of spring. Others consider starting their own annuals from seed one of the most rewarding aspects of gardening. Both methods have benefits, and many gardeners use a combination of the two.

Purchasing plants is usually easier than starting from seed and provides you with plants that are well grown and often already in bloom. Starting seeds can be impractical. It requires space, facilities and time. Some seeds require specific conditions difficult to achieve in a house, or they have erratic germination rates. Other seeds, however, are easy and inexpensive to start. Starting from seed offers you a greater selection because seed catalogs list many more plants than are offered at most garden centers. Growing annuals from seed is discussed on pp. 26–29.

Purchased annuals are grown in a variety of containers. Some are sold in individual pots, some in divided cell-packs and others in undivided trays. Each type has its advantages and disadvantages.

Annuals in **individual pots** are usually well established and have plenty of space for root growth. These annuals were probably seeded in flat trays and then transplanted into individual pots once they developed a few leaves. The cost of labor, pots and soil can make this option somewhat more expensive. If you are planting a large area you may also find it difficult to transport large numbers of plants of this size.

Annuals grown in **cell-packs** are often inexpensive and hold several plants, making them easy to transport. These annuals suffer less root damage when transplanted than do annuals in undivided trays, but because each cell is quite small, plants may become root-bound quickly.

Annuals grown in **undivided trays** are also inexpensive. They have plenty of room for root growth and can be left in the trays longer than can plants in other types of containers. Their roots, however, tend to become entangled, making the plants difficult to separate.

Regardless of the type of container, the best plants to choose are often those not yet flowering. These plants are younger and are less likely to be root-bound. Check for roots emerging from the holes at the bottom of the cells, or gently remove the plant from the container to look at the roots. An overabundance of roots means that the plant is too mature for the container, especially if the roots are wrapped around the inside of the container in a thick web. Such plants are slow to establish once they are transplanted into the garden.

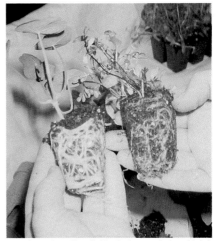

Root-bound seedling (left), nicely rooted plant (right)

Plants should be compact and have good color. Healthy leaves look firm and vibrant. Unhealthy leaves may be discolored, chewed or wilted. Tall, leggy plants have likely been deprived of light. Sickly plants may not survive being transplanted and may spread pests or diseases to the rest of your garden.

Once you get your annuals home, water them if they are dry. Annuals growing in small containers may require water more than once a day. See p. 30 for information on planting out your new annuals.

Calibrachoa (center) and angel wings (below) are purchased as bedding plants.

ANNUALS FROM SEED

Starting annuals from seed can be fun and will provide you with a wider variety of plants than those available at a garden center. Dozens of catalogs from different growers offer a diverse selection of annuals that you can start from seed. Many gardeners while away their winter evenings by poring through seed catalogs and planning their spring and summer gardens.

Starting your own annuals can save you money, particularly if you have a large area to plant. The basic equipment necessary is not expensive, and most seeds can be started in a sunny window. You may, however, have limited space. One or two trays of annuals don't take up too much room, but storing more than that may be unreasonable. For this reason, many gardeners start a few specialty plants themselves but purchase the bulk of their annuals already started from a garden center.

Each plant entry in this book will have specific information on starting the annual from seed, but some basic procedures apply to all seeds.

The easiest way for the home gardener to start seeds is in cell-packs in trays with plastic dome covers. The cell-packs keep roots separated, and the tray and dome keep moisture in.

Seeds can also be started in peat pots or peat pellets. The advantage to starting in peat pots or pellets is that you won't disturb the roots when transplanting your annuals. When planting peat pots into the garden, be sure to remove the top couple of inches of pot. If any of the pot sticks up out of the soil, it can wick moisture away from your plant. It is also advisable to slice vertically down each side of the peat pot or pellet to ensure the roots will be able to grow out into the soil.

Another seeding method that involves minimal root disturbance is to start the seeds in 4" pots. When it is time to plant, dig a hole, place the pot in the ground and then backfill around the pot.

Preparing seed trays

Using folded paper to plant small seeds

Lift the pot out of the ground, then gently remove the plant and rootball from the pot. Set the plant into the pre-shaped hole, and water to settle the soil around the rootball. This method works very well as long as the plants are not root-bound.

Use a soil mix that is intended for seedlings. These mixes are very fine, usually made from peat moss, vermiculite and perlite. The mix will have good water-holding capacity and will have been sterilized to prevent pests and diseases from attacking your tender young seedlings. Using a sterile soil mix, keeping soil evenly moist and maintaining good air circulation will prevent the problem of **damping-off**. Damping-off is caused by a variety of soil-borne fungi, and the affected seedling will appear to have been pinched at soil level. The pinched area blackens, and the seedling topples over and dies. Damping-off can also be reduced or prevented by spreading a $1/4$" layer of peat moss over the seedbed.

Fill your pots, cell-packs or seed trays with the soil mix and firm it down slightly. Soil that is too firmly packed will not drain well. Wet the soil before planting your seeds to prevent them from getting washed around.

Large seeds can be planted one or two to a cell, but smaller seeds may have to be placed in a folded piece of paper and sprinkled evenly over the soil surface. Very tiny seeds, like those of begonias, can be mixed with fine sand before being sprinkled evenly across the soil surface.

Small seeds will not need to be covered with any more soil, but medium-sized seeds can be lightly covered, and large seeds can be poked into the soil. Seeds of some plants (noted as such in the individual entries) need to be exposed to light in order to germinate. These seeds should be left on the soil surface regardless of their size.

Place pots or flats of seeds in clear plastic bags to retain humidity while the seeds are germinating. Many planting trays come with clear plastic covers, which can be placed over the trays to keep the moisture in. Remove the plastic once the seeds have germinated. You should check the progress of your seedlings daily.

Water seeds and small seedlings with a fine spray from a hand-held mister.

Watering seeds with a mister

Prepared seed tray

Sprouted seedlings with fluorescent light

Small seeds can easily be washed around if the spray is too strong. The amount and timing of watering is critical to successfully growing annuals from seed. Most germinated seeds and young seedlings will perish if the soil is allowed to dry out. Strive to maintain a consistently moist soil, which may mean watering lightly as often as two to three times a day, if necessary. As the seedlings get bigger, you can cut back on the number of times you have to water, but you will have to water a little more heavily. Generally, when the seedlings have their first true leaves (those that look like the adult leaves), you can cut back to watering once a day.

Small seedlings will not need to be fertilized until they have about four or five true leaves. Seeds provide all the energy and nutrients that younger seedlings require. Fertilizer will cause the plants to develop soft growth that is more susceptible to insects and diseases, and too strong a fertilizer can burn tender young roots. When the first leaves that sprouted (seed leaves) begin to shrivel, the plant has used up all its seed energy, so you can begin to apply a fertilizer diluted to one-quarter the usual strength.

Seedlings are big enough to transplant when the first true leaves appear. If the seedlings get too big for their containers before you are ready to plant in your garden, you may have to transplant them to larger pots to prevent them from becoming root-bound.

Harden plants off by exposing them to sunnier, windier conditions and fluctuating outdoor temperatures for increasing periods of time every day for at least a week. A cold frame is ideal for hardening plants off. It can also be used to protect tender plants over the winter, to start seeds early in winter and spring and to start seeds that need a cold treatment (if your area gets cold enough). See our book *Perennials for Illinois* for additional information about cold frames.

Some annuals, such as those with large or quick-germinating seeds or those that are difficult to transplant, can be sown directly in the garden. Start with a well-prepared bed that has been smoothly raked. The small furrows left by the rake will help hold moisture and prevent the seeds from being washed away. Sprinkle the seeds onto the soil and cover them lightly with peat moss or more soil. Larger seeds can be planted slightly deeper into the soil. You may not want to sow very tiny seeds directly in the garden because they can blow or wash away.

The soil should be kept moist to ensure even germination. Use a gentle spray to avoid washing the seeds around the bed, or they may pool into dense clumps. Cover your newly seeded bed with chicken wire, an old sheet or some thorny branches to discourage pets from digging. A row cover also discourages animals and helps speed germination. Remove the cover once the seeds have germinated.

ANNUALS FOR DIRECT SEEDING

- Agrostemma
- Amaranth
- Baby's breath
- Bachelor's buttons
- Bidens
- Black-eyed Susan
- Calendula
- Cosmos
- Creeping zinnia
- Hyacinth bean
- Larkspur
- Lavatera
- Nasturtium
- Phlox
- Poppy
- Rose-of-heaven
- Sunflower
- Sweet pea
- Xeranthemum
- Zinnia

Agrostemma (above)

Phlox (center), poppy (below)

PLANTING ANNUALS

If your new plants have been growing in a greenhouse, they need to be hardened off before being transplanted into the garden. Place them outdoors in light shade each day and bring them into a sheltered porch, garage or house at night for about a week. This procedure will acclimatize them to your environment.

Once your annuals are hardened off, it is time to transplant. If you have already prepared your beds (see p. 22), you are ready to start. The only tool you'll be likely to need is a trowel. Set aside enough time to complete the job, to avoid removing plants from their pots and then not planting them. If young plants are left out in the sun, they can quickly dry out and die. It's better to plant in the early morning, in the evening or on an overcast day.

Moisten the soil to help ease the plants from their containers. Push on the bottom of the cell or pot with your thumb to remove the plants. If the plants were growing in an undivided tray, you will have to gently untangle the roots. Very tangled roots can be separated by immersing them in water and washing off some soil. If you must handle the plant, hold it by a leaf to avoid crushing the stems. Remove and discard any damaged growth.

The rootball should contain a network of white plant roots. If the rootball is densely matted and twisted (root-bound), score the rootball vertically on four sides with a sharp knife or gently break it apart in order to encourage the roots to extend and grow outward. New root growth will start from the cuts or breaks, allowing the plant to spread outwards.

Insert your trowel into the soil and pull it toward you, creating a wedge. Place your annual into the hole and firm the soil around the plant with your hands. Water newly planted annuals gently but thoroughly. They need frequent watering for a couple of weeks, until they establish.

You don't have to be conservative when arranging your garden beds.

Though formal bedding-out patterns are still used in many parks and formal gardens, there are more design choices than simple, straight rows. Today's plantings are often made in casual groups and natural drifts. The quickest way to space out your annuals is to remove them from their containers and randomly place them on the bed. You will get a nice mix of colors and plants without too much planning. Prevent the roots from drying out by planting only one small section at a time, particularly if you have a large bed to plant.

Formal planting (above)

If you are adding just a few annuals here and there to accent your shrub and perennial plantings, then plant in groups. Random clusters of three to five annuals add color and interest. Always plant groups of the same annual in odd numbers for a more natural effect. One technique used by some landscapers is called 'three rock.' Turn your back to the landscape and toss three shiny rocks behind you. Place the plants where the rocks landed. This technique can be used with five or seven rocks as well.

Combine low-growing or spreading annuals with tall or bushy ones. Keep the tallest plants toward the back and smallest plants toward the front of each bed. This arrangement improves the visibility of the plants and hides the often unattractive lower parts of taller plants. Be sure to leave your plants enough room to spread. They may look lonely and far apart when you first plant them, but annuals quickly grow to fill in the space you leave.

We suggest spacing distances in each plant entry. A good rule of thumb for annuals is to space slightly less than the plant's spread, to give a pleasing, full

Annuals nicely arranged according to height

effect when the plants mature. Some plants need more space between them to encourage good air circulation. This situation is also noted in the appropriate plant entries.

Aside from these general guidelines, there are no strict rules when it comes to planting and spacing. Plant your annuals the way you like them, whether it is in straight rows or in a jumble of colors, shapes and sizes. The idea is to have fun and to create something that you will enjoy for the rest of the season.

CARING FOR ANNUALS

Ongoing maintenance will keep your garden looking its best. Some annuals require more care than others do, but most require minimal care once established. Weeding, watering, fertilizing, pinching and deadheading are the basic tasks that, when performed regularly, pay dividends throughout the season. As well, some perennials grown as annuals may be overwintered with little effort.

Deadheading dahlias

Weeding

Controlling weed populations keeps the garden healthy and neat. Weeding may not be anyone's favorite task, but it is essential. Weeds compete with your plants for light, nutrients and space, and they can also harbor pests and diseases.

Weeds can be pulled by hand or with a hoe. It is easiest to pull weeds shortly after a rainfall, when the soil is soft and damp. A hoe scuffed quickly across the soil surface will uproot small weeds and sever larger ones from their roots. Try to pull weeds while they are still small. Once they are large enough to flower, many will quickly set seed, and then you will have an entire new generation to worry about.

Mulching

A layer of mulch around your plants will prevent weeds from germinating by preventing sufficient light from reaching their seeds. Those that do germinate will be smothered or will find it difficult to get to the soil surface, exhausting their energy before they get a chance to grow. Weeds are very easy to pull from a mulched bed.

Mulch also helps maintain consistent soil temperatures and allows the soil to better retain moisture, which means you will not need to water as much. In areas that receive heavy wind or rainfall, mulch can protect soil and prevent erosion. Mulching is effective in both garden beds and planters and is especially important where summer temperatures can climb to over 90° F.

Organic mulches include compost, bark chips, grass clippings and shredded leaves. These mulches add nutrients to soil as they break down, improving the quality of the soil and ultimately the health of your plants. Shredded newspaper also makes wonderful mulch. Use only newsprint and not glossy paper. Shredded cedar bark has the advantage of containing a naturally occurring fungicide, which can help prevent root rot.

Spread mulch a couple of inches deep over the soil after you have planted your annuals. As your mulch breaks down over summer, be sure to replenish it. Don't pile the mulch too thickly in the area immediately around the crowns and stems of your annuals. Mulch that is too close to plants traps moisture, prevents air circulation and encourages fungal disease.

Weeds & tools (above)

Watering

Once your annuals are established, water thoroughly but infrequently, making sure the water penetrates at least 4" into the soil. Annuals given a sprinkle of water every day develop roots that stay close to the soil surface, making the plants vulnerable to heat and dry spells. Annuals given a deep watering once a week develop a deeper root system. In a dry spell they will be adapted to seeking out the water trapped deeper in the ground.

To prevent needless water loss to evaporation, apply mulch, and do most of your watering in the morning. Morning, rather than evening, watering allows any moisture on the plants to dry during the day, thereby lessening the risk of fungal disease.

Mulched garden

To avoid overwatering, check the amount of moisture in the rootzone before applying any water. Poke your finger into the top one to two inches of soil. You can also try rolling a bit of soil from around the plant into a ball. Moist soil will form a ball, and no extra water is needed.

To save time, money and water, you may wish to install an irrigation system. Irrigation systems apply the water exactly where it is needed, near the roots, and reduce the amount of water lost to evaporation. They can be very complex or very simple, depending on your needs. A simple irrigation system would involve laying soaker hoses around your garden beds under the mulch. Consult with your local garden centers or landscape professionals for more information.

Hanging baskets & containers need to be watered regularly.

Annuals in hanging baskets and planters will probably need to be watered more frequently than plants growing in the ground. The smaller the container, the more often the plants will need watering. Containers and hanging moss baskets may need to be watered twice daily during hot, sunny weather. If the soil in your container dries out, you will have to water several times to make sure water is absorbed throughout the planting medium. Dig into the soil, and if it is dry at all, water more. Your local garden center should carry wetting agents, such as Water-In, that can help water penetrate into dry soils. These products are often added to peat moss and soil mixes to improve their water-holding abilities.

Fertilizing

Many annuals will flower most profusely if they are fertilized regularly. Some gardeners fertilize hanging baskets and container gardens every time they water, using a very dilute fertilizer so as not to burn the roots. Too much fertilizer, however, can result in weak plant growth that is susceptible to pest and disease problems. Some plants, such as nasturtiums, grow better without fertilizer and may produce few or no flowers when fertilized excessively.

Fertilizer comes in various forms. Liquids and water-soluble powders are the easiest to use when watering. Slow-release pellets or granules are mixed into the garden or potting soil or sprinkled around the plant and left to work through the summer.

Your local garden center should carry a good selection of fertilizers. Follow the directions on the containers carefully because using too much fertilizer can kill your plants by burning their roots. Whenever possible, use organic rather than chemical fertilizers because organic types are generally less concentrated and less likely to burn your plants.

Organic fertilizers feed the soil, not just the plant roots. Healthy soil allows plants to grow better over the course of the summer. Organic fertilizers don't work as quickly as inorganic fertilizers, but they don't leach out as quickly either. Organic fertilizers can be watered into soil or used as a foliar spray as often as weekly.

If you look for the fertilizer numbers on labels, organics will usually have lower N : P : K numbers (Nitrogen : Phosphorus : Potassium ratios) than chemical fertilizers. The labels should list the ingredients. Organic fertilizers can be simple or complex formulations of any or all of the following: alfalfa pellets, dehydrated manure, animal tankage, crab meal, coco meal, corn gluten, dried blood, kelp meal, alfalfa meal, sunflower meal, cottonseed meal, greensand, rock phosphate, humus and gypsum. Chemical fertilizers often include such compounds as ammonium phosphate, potassium phosphate, boric acid, ammonium sulfate and triple superphosphate. Organic fertilizers, with their lower nutrient ratios and ingredients from natural sources, do not disrupt the microorganism balance in the soil to the same extent that chemical fertilizers do.

Many of the ingredients in organic fertilizers are available separately. You can purchase different components and make your own concoction, or use them individually. Products to use on their own include bonemeal, touted as a wonderful fertilizer for bulbs; liquid fish emulsion; and alfalfa pellets, which

Fuchsia (top) & petunia appreciate regular fertilizing.

contain triacontanol, a very powerful plant growth hormone that stimulates the roots to better use the fertilizer that is applied. Bonemeal and fish emulsion may attract unwanted garden visitors that can cause major destruction. If you have problems with small mammal pests, mix any added bonemeal well with the soil rather than using a handful at the bottom of the planting hole. Fish emulsion can be diluted to reduce the varmint-attracting aroma.

Spiral stakes

Grooming

Good grooming helps keep your annuals healthy and neat, makes them flower more profusely and prevents many pest and disease problems. Grooming may include pinching, trimming, staking and deadheading.

Pinching refers to removing by hand, or with scissors, any straggly growth and the tips of leggy annuals. Plants in cell-packs may develop tall and straggly growth in an attempt to get light. Pinch back the long growth when transplanting to encourage bushier growth. Also remove any yellow or dying leaves.

If annuals appear tired and withered by mid-summer, try **trimming** them back to encourage a second bloom. Mounding or low-growing annuals, such as petunias, respond well to trimming. Take your garden shears and trim back a quarter or half of the plant growth. New growth will sprout along with a second flush of flowers. Give the plants a light fertilizing as well at this time.

Some annuals have very tall growth and cannot be pinched or trimmed. Instead, remove the main shoot after it blooms, and side shoots may develop.

Tall annuals, such as larkspur, may require **staking** with bamboo or other tall, thin stakes. Tie the plant loosely to the stake—strips of nylon hosiery make soft ties that won't cut into the plant. Make sure the strips are narrow so as not to show. Stake bushy plants with twiggy branches or tomato cages. Insert the twigs or cages around the plant when it is small, and it will grow to fill in and hide the supports.

Deadheading, or removing faded flowers, tidies plants and often helps prolong their bloom. It also helps keep annuals healthy because decaying flowers can harbor pests and diseases. To save yourself a big job later, get into the habit of picking off spent flowers as you are looking around your garden. Some plants, such as impatiens and wax begonia, are self-cleaning or self-grooming, meaning that they drop their faded blossoms on their own.

Impatiens are self-cleaning annuals.

Growing Perennials as Annuals

Many plants grown as annuals are actually perennials, such as geraniums (genus *Pelargonium*), that are native to warm climates and are unable to survive our colder winters. Other plants grown as annuals are biennials, such as Canterbury bells, and are started very early in the year to allow them to grow and flower in a single season. These perennials and biennials are indicated as such in the plant entries. You can use several techniques to keep these plants for more than one summer.

Perennials with tuberous roots, such as dahlias, can be dug up in fall, after the plant dies back, and replanted in late winter or early spring. If there is a chance that the ground may freeze, dig up the tubers before that can happen. Shake the loose dirt from the roots and let them dry in a cool dark place. Once dry, the rest of the soil should brush away. Dust the tubers with an antifungal powder, such as garden sulfur (found at garden centers), before storing them in moist peat moss or coarse sawdust. Keep them in a cool, dark, dry place that doesn't freeze. If they start to sprout, pot them and keep them in moist soil in a bright window. They should be potted by late winter or early spring so that they will be ready for planting in spring.

Cuttings can be taken from large or fast-growing plants such as black-eyed Susan vine. Grow late-summer cuttings over the winter for new spring plants. Cuttings are also a good idea for seed-grown plants that have developed unique foliage or other features not likely to be replicated with a new batch of seeds. See our book *Perennials for Illinois* for information on taking and growing cuttings.

If winter storage sounds like too much work, replace your annuals each year and leave the hard work to the growers.

Geranium

Black-eyed Susan vine

Problems & Pests

New annuals are planted each spring, and often different species are grown each year. These factors make it difficult for pests and diseases to find their preferred host plants and establish a population. On the other hand, because annual species are often grown together in masses, any problems that do set in over the summer may attack all the plants.

For many years, pest control meant spraying or dusting with the goal to eliminate every pest in the landscape. A more moderate approach advocated today is known as IPM (Integrated Pest Management or Integrated Plant Management). The goal of IPM is to reduce pest damage to negligible levels.

You must determine what degree of damage is acceptable to you. Consider whether a pest's damage is localized or covers the entire plant. Will the damage being done kill the plant or is it affecting only the outward appearance? Are there methods of controlling the pest without chemicals? For an interesting overview of IPM, consult the University of Illinois Extension website at

<http://www.ipm.uiuc.edu/ipm/index.html>.

An effective and responsible pest-management program has four steps. Cultural controls are the most important. Physical controls should be attempted next, followed by biological controls. Resort to chemical controls only when the first three possibilities have been exhausted.

Cultural controls are the gardening techniques you use in the day-to-day care of your garden. Perhaps the best defense against pests and diseases is to grow annuals in the conditions for which they are suited. It is also very important to keep your soil healthy, with plenty of organic matter.

Other cultural controls are equally simple and straightforward. Choose resistant varieties of annuals that are not prone to problems. Space your plants so that they have good air circulation in and around them and are not stressed from competing for light, nutrients and space. Remove plants that are decimated by the same pests every year. Dispose of diseased foliage and branches. Prevent the spread of disease by keeping your gardening tools clean and by tidying up fallen leaves and dead plant matter at the end of every growing season.

Physical controls are generally used to combat insect and mammal problems. An example of such a control is picking insects off plants by hand, which is not as daunting as it may seem if you catch the problem when it is just beginning. Large, slow insects such as Japanese beetles are particularly easy to pick off. Other physical controls include traps, barriers, scarecrows and natural repellants that make a plant taste or smell bad to pests. Garden centers offer a wide array of such devices. Physical control of diseases usually involves removing the infected plant or parts of the plant to keep the problem from spreading.

Biological controls make use of populations of natural predators. Such animals as birds, snakes, frogs, spiders, lady beetles and certain bacteria help keep pest populations at a manageable level. Encourage these creatures to take up permanent residence in your garden. A birdbath and birdfeeder will encourage birds to enjoy your yard and feed on a wide variety of insect pests. Many beneficial insects are probably already living in your garden, and you can encourage them to stay and multiply by planting appropriate food sources. For example, many beneficial insects eat nectar from flowers such as daisies and the perennial yarrow.

Another form of biological control is B.t. (the soil bacterium *Bacillus thuringiensis* var. *kurstaki)*, which breaks down the gut lining of some insect pests. It is commonly available in garden centers.

Chemical controls should be used only as a last resort because they can do more harm than good. The main drawback to using any chemical is that it may also kill the beneficial insects you

Frogs eat many insect pests.

have been trying to attract. If, however, you have tried cultural, physical and biological methods and still wish to take further action, call your local University of Illinois Extension office to obtain a list of chemicals recommended for particular diseases or insects.

Try to use 'organic' types, available at most garden centers. Organic sprays are no less dangerous than chemical ones, but they will at least break down into harmless compounds eventually. Consumers are demanding effective pest products that do not harm the environment, and less toxic, more precisely targeted pesticides are becoming available. See also the benign alternatives listed in the next section.

Take care when using chemicals to follow the manufacturer's instructions and apply only in the recommended amounts. A large amount of insecticide is not any more effective in controlling pests than the recommended amount. Note that if a particular pest is not listed on the package, it will not be controlled by that product. Proper and early identification of pests is vital to finding a quick solution.

Whereas cultural, physical, biological and chemical controls are all possible defenses against insects, diseases can be controlled only culturally. It is most often weakened plants that succumb to diseases. Healthy plants can often fight off illness although some diseases can infect plants regardless of their level of health. Prevention, most often through cultural means, is often the only hope. Once an annual has been infected, it should be destroyed to prevent the disease from spreading.

Pest Control Alternatives

The following common-sense treatments for pests and diseases allow the gardener a measure of control without resorting to toxic fungicides and pesticides.

ANT CONTROL
Mix 3 c. water, 1 c. white sugar and 4 tsp. liquid boric acid in a pot. Bring this mix just to a boil and remove from heat. Let the mix cool, then pour small amounts into bottlecaps and place them around the ant-infested area. Alternatively, try setting out a mixture of equal parts powdered borax and icing sugar (no water).

ANTITRANSPIRANTS
These products reduce transpiration, or loss of water, from plants. The waxy polymers also surround fungal spores, preventing their spread to surrounding leaves and stems. Applied according to label directions, antitranspirants are environmentally friendly.

BAKING SODA & HORTICULTURAL OIL SPRAY
This mixture is effective for powdery mildew. In a spray bottle, mix 4 tsp. baking soda, 1 tbsp. horticultural oil and 1 gal. water. Spray the foliage lightly, including the undersides. Do not pour or spray this mix directly onto soil.

COFFEE GROUNDS SPRAY

Boil 2 lb. coffee grounds in 3 gal. water for about 10 minutes. Allow to cool; strain the grounds out. Apply as a spray to reduce problems with whiteflies.

COMPOST TEA

Mix 1–2 lb. compost in 5 gal. of water. Let sit for four to seven days. Dilute the mix until it resembles weak tea. Use during normal watering or apply as a foliar spray to prevent or treat fungal diseases.

FISH EMULSION OR SEAWEED (KELP)

These products are usually used as foliar nutrient feeds, but they appear to also work against fungal diseases either by preventing the fungus from spreading to noninfected areas or by changing the growing conditions for the fungus.

GARLIC SPRAY

This spray is an effective, organic means of controlling aphids, leafhoppers, whiteflies and some fungi and nematodes. Soak 6 tbsp. finely minced garlic in 2 tsp. mineral oil for at least 24 hours. Add 1 pt. of water and $1^1/2$ tsp. of liquid dish soap. Stir and strain into a glass container for storage. Combine 1–2 tbsp. of this concentrate with 2 c. water to make a spray. Test the spray on a couple of leaves and check after two days. If there is no damage, spray infested plants thoroughly, ensuring good coverage of the foliage.

HORTICULTURAL OIL SPRAY

Mix 5 tbsp. horticultural oil per 1 gal. of water, and apply as a spray for a variety of insect and fungal problems.

INSECTICIDAL SOAP

Mix 1 tsp. of mild dish detergent or pure soap (biodegradable options are available) with 1 qt. of water in a clean spray bottle. Spray surfaces of insect-infested plants and rinse well within an hour to avoid foliage discoloration.

MILK SPRAY

Milk spray helps prevent and control mildew and other fungal diseases. It has been tested on roses and a variety of vegetables, with moderate success. Mix one part milk with nine parts water and apply as a spray every five to seven days for a total of three applications. Low-fat milk is recommended for less odor.

NEEM OIL

Neem oil is derived from the neem tree (native to India) and is used as an insecticide, miticide and fungicide. It is most effective when used preventively. Apply when conditions are favorable for disease development. Neem does not harm most beneficial insects and microorganisms.

SULFUR AND LIME-SULFUR

These products help prevent fungal diseases. You can purchase ready-made products or wettable powders you mix yourself. Do not spray when the temperature is expected to be 90° F or higher, or plants may be damaged.

Glossary of Pests & Diseases

APHIDS

Tiny, pear-shaped insects, winged or wingless; green, black, brown, red or gray. Cluster along stems, on buds and on leaves. Suck sap from plants; cause distorted or stunted growth. Sticky honeydew forms on surfaces and encourages sooty mold.

What to Do: Squish small colonies by hand; dislodge them with water spray; spray serious infestations with insecticidal soap, horticultural oil or neem oil (see previous section or package directions); encourage predatory insects and birds that feed on aphids.

ASTER YELLOWS

see Viruses

BEETLES

Many types and sizes; usually rounded in shape with hard, shell-like outer wings covering membranous inner wings. Some are beneficial, e.g., ladybird beetles ('ladybugs'); others, e.g., June beetles, flea beetles, leaf skeletonizers and weevils, eat plants. Larvae: see Borers, Grubs. Both adult beetles and larvae chew small or large holes in or around margins of leaves; consume entire leaves or areas between leaf veins ('skeletonize'); may also chew holes in flowers.

What to Do: Pick beetles off at night and drop them into an old coffee can half filled with soapy water (soap prevents them from floating); spread an old sheet under plants and shake off beetles to collect and dispose of them. Can use a handheld vacuum cleaner to remove them from plant. Parasitic nematodes are effective if beetle goes through part of its life cycle in the ground.

BLIGHT

Fungal diseases, many types; e.g., leaf blight, needle blight, snow blight. Leaves, stems and flowers blacken, rot and die.

What to Do: Thin stems to improve air circulation; keep mulch away from base of plants; remove debris from garden at end of growing season. Remove and destroy infected plant parts.

BORERS

Larvae of some moths, wasps, beetles; among the most damaging plant pests. Worm-like; vary in size and get bigger as they bore through plants. Burrow into stems, leaves and/or roots; destroy conducting tissue and structural strength. Weakened stems break; leaves wilt; may see tunnels in leaves, stems or

Aphids

Japanese beetles

Lygus bug

roots; underground parts may be hollowed out entirely or in part.

What to Do: May be able to squish borers within leaves. Remove and destroy bored parts; may need to dig up and destroy infected roots and rhizomes.

BUGS (TRUE BUGS)

Small insects, up to $1/2$" long; green, brown, black or brightly colored and patterned. Many beneficial; a few pierce plants to suck out sap. Toxins may be injected that deform plants; sunken areas left where pierced; leaves rip as they grow; leaves, buds and new growth may be dwarfed and deformed.

What to Do: Remove debris and weeds from around plants in fall to destroy overwintering sites. Pick off by hand and drop into soapy water. Use parasitic nematodes if part of bug's life cycle is in the ground. Spray plants with insecticidal soap or neem oil (see previous section or package directions).

CATERPILLARS

Larvae of butterflies, moths, sawflies. Include budworms, cutworms (see Cutworms), leaf rollers, leaf tiers, loopers. Chew foliage and buds; can completely defoliate a plant if infestation severe.

What to Do: Removal from plant is best control. Use high-pressure water and soap, or pick caterpillars off by hand. Control biologically using B.t.

CUTWORMS

Larvae of some moths. Smooth-skinned, plump caterpillars about 1" long; curl up when disturbed. Usually affect young plants and seedlings, which may be completely consumed or chewed off at base.

What to Do: Pick off by hand. Create physical barriers by using toilet tissue tubes to make collars around plant bases; push tubes at least halfway into ground. Or insert three toothpicks into soil around each plant, making sure toothpicks are right up against stem.

DAMPING-OFF
see p. 27

GRAY MOLD (BOTRYTIS BLIGHT)

Fungal disease. Leaves, stems and flowers blacken, rot and die.

What to Do: Thin stems to improve air circulation, keep mulch away from base of plant, particularly in spring when plant starts to sprout; remove debris from garden at end of growing season; do not overwater. Remove and destroy any infected plant parts. Use horticultural oil or compost tea as a preventive measure.

GRUBS

Larvae of different beetles, commonly found below soil level; usually curled in C-shape. Body white or gray; head may be white, gray, brown or reddish. Problematic in lawns; may feed on plant roots. Plant wilts despite regular watering; may pull easily out of ground in severe cases.

What to Do: Toss any grubs found when digging onto pavement for birds to devour; apply parasitic nematodes.

LEAFHOPPERS

Small, wedge-shaped insects; can be green, brown, gray or multi-colored. Jump around frantically when disturbed. Suck juice from leaves, cause distorted growth, carry diseases such as aster yellows.

What to Do: Encourage predators by planting nectar-producing species such as yarrow. Wash insects off with strong spray of water; spray with insecticidal soap or neem oil (see previous section or package directions).

LEAF MINERS

Tiny, stubby larvae of some butterflies and moths; may be yellow or green. Tunnel within leaves leaving winding trails that are lighter in color than rest of leaf. Unsightly rather than health risk to plant.

What to Do: Remove debris from area in fall to destroy overwintering sites; attract parasitic wasps with nectar plants such as yarrow. Remove and destroy infected foliage; can sometimes squish by hand within leaf. Floating row covers prevent eggs from being laid on plant. Bright blue sticky cards, available in most garden centers and through mail order, attract and trap adult leaf miners.

LEAF SKELETONIZERS
see Beetles

LEAF SPOT

Two common types: one caused by bacteria and one by fungi. *Bacterial:* small brown or purple speckles grow to encompass entire leaves; leaves may drop. *Fungal:* black, brown or yellow spots; leaves wither; e.g., scab, tar spot, leaf blotch.

What to Do: Bacterial infection more severe; must remove entire plant. For fungal infection, remove and destroy infected plant parts. Sterilize removal tools; avoid wetting foliage or touching wet foliage; remove and destroy debris at end of growing season. Compost tea often works, or can spray plant with liquid copper.

MEALYBUGS

Tiny crawling insects related to aphids; appear to be covered with white fuzz or flour. More often found on houseplants than in the garden. Sucking damage stunts and stresses plant. Mealybugs excrete honeydew, promoting sooty mold.

What to Do: Remove by hand from smaller plants; wash plant off with soap and water; wipe off with alcohol-soaked swabs; remove heavily infested leaves; encourage or introduce natural predators such as mealybug destroyer beetle and parasitic wasps; spray with insecticidal soap. *Note:* larvae of mealybug destroyer beetles look like very large mealybugs. Always check plants for mealybugs before buying.

Leaf miner damage

Powdery mildew

MILDEW

Two types, both caused by a fungus. *Downy mildew:* yellow spots on upper sides of leaves and downy fuzz on undersides; fuzz may be yellow, white or gray. *Powdery mildew:* leaves have white or gray powdery coating that doesn't brush off.

What to Do: Choose resistant cultivars; space plants well; thin stems to encourage air circulation; tidy garden debris in fall. Remove and destroy infected leaves or other parts. Spray compost tea or highly diluted fish emulsion (1 tsp. per qt. of water) to control downy and powdery mildew. For powdery mildew, spray foliage with baking soda and horticultural oil (see previous section); three applications one week apart.

MITES

Tiny, eight-legged relatives of spiders without their insect-eating habits. Examples: spider mites, rust mites, thread-footed mites. Invisible or nearly invisible to naked eye; red, yellow, green or translucent; usually found on undersides of plant leaves. Suck juice out of leaves; may see their fine webs on leaves and stems; may see mites moving on leaf undersides; leaves become discolored and speckled in appearance, then turn brown and shrivel.

What to Do: Wash off with strong spray of water daily until all signs of infestation are gone; predatory mites that attack plant-eating mites are available through garden centers; apply insecticidal soap, horticultural oil or neem oil (see previous section or package directions).

MOSAIC

see Viruses

NEMATODES

Tiny worms that give plants disease symptoms. One type infects foliage and stems; the other infects roots. *Foliar:* yellow spots that turn brown on leaves; leaves shrivel and wither; problem starts on lowest leaves and works up plant. *Root-knot:* plant is stunted, may wilt; yellow spots on leaves; roots have tiny bumps or knots.

What to Do: Mulch soil, add organic matter, clean up debris in fall, add parasitic nematodes to soil to attack plant-eating nematodes. Don't touch wet foliage of infected plants. Remove infected plants in extreme cases.

ROT

Several different fungi or bacteria that affect different parts of the plant and can kill plant. *Black rot:* bacterial; enters through pores or small wounds. Begins as V-shaped lesions along leaf margins. Leaf veins turn black and eventually plant dies. *Crown rot (stem rot):* fungal; affects base of plant, causing stems to blacken and fall over and leaves to yellow and wilt. *Root rot:* fungal; leaves yellow and plant wilts; digging up plant shows roots rotted away.

What to Do: Keep soil well drained; don't damage plant when digging around it; keep mulches away from plant base. Remove infected plants.

RUST

Fungi. Pale spots on upper leaf surfaces; orange, fuzzy or dusty spots underneath.

What to Do: Choose rust-resistant varieties and cultivars; avoid handling wet leaves; provide plant with good air circulation; use horticultural oil to protect new foliage; clean up garden debris at end of season. Remove and destroy infected plant parts. Don't put infected plants in compost.

SCALE INSECTS

Tiny, shelled insects that suck sap, weakening and possibly killing plant or making it vulnerable to other problems. Scale appears as tiny bumps, typically along stems or on undersides of leaves. Once female scale insect has pierced plant with mouthpart, it is there for life. Juvenile scale insects are called crawlers.

What to Do: Wipe off with alcohol-soaked swabs; spray with water to dislodge crawlers; prune out heavily infested branches; encourage natural predators and parasites; spray dormant oil in spring before bud break.

SLUGS & SNAILS

Slugs lack shells; snails have spiral shells. Both are mollusks with slimy, smooth skin; can be up to 8" long; gray, green, black, beige, yellow or spotted.

Slug

Mosaic virus

Leave large ragged holes in foliage and silvery slime trails on and around plants. Slugs are more problematic than snails in Illinois.

What to Do: Remove slug habitat including garden debris or mulches around plant bases. Increase air circulation. Pick off by hand in the evening and squish with boot or drop in can of soapy water. Spread diatomaceous earth (available in garden centers) on soil around plants; it will pierce their soft bodies and cause them to dehydrate. **Do not** use the diatomaceous earth that is intended for swimming pool filters. Slug and snail baits, also available at local garden centers, are effective; some new formulations are nontoxic to children and pets. Beer in a shallow dish may be effective. Attach strips of copper to wood around raised beds or to smaller boards inserted around plants; slugs and snails get shocked if they touch copper surfaces.

SMUT

Fungus that attacks any above-ground plant parts, including leaves, stems and flowers. Forms fleshy white galls that turn black and powdery.

What to Do: Remove and destroy infected plants. Avoid placing same plants in that spot for next few years.

Annuals prone to slug and snail damage should not be mulched, to avoid providing habitat for the pests. Fortunately, some of these annuals may not need mulching in any case. For example, hostas may shade the soil sufficiently to limit weed competition on their own. Alternatively, use slug-repellant mulches, such as cedar chips, pine needles and crushed egg shells.

SOOTY MOLD

Fungus. Thin black film forms on leaf surfaces and reduces amount of light getting through.

What to Do: Wipe mold off leaf surfaces; control insects such as aphids, mealybugs, whiteflies (honeydew they deposit on leaves encourages mold).

SPIDER MITES
see Mites

THRIPS

Tiny insects, difficult to see; may be visible if you disturb them by blowing gently on an infested flower. Yellow, black or brown, with narrow, fringed wings. Suck juice out of plant cells, particularly in flowers and buds, causing gray-mottled petals and leaves, dying buds and distorted, stunted growth.

What to Do: Remove and destroy infected plant parts; encourage native predatory insects with nectar plants such as yarrow; spray severe infestations with insecticidal soap or with horticultural oil at 5 tbsp. per gal. Use sticky blue cards to attract and trap adults.

VIRUSES

Plant may be stunted and leaves and flowers distorted, streaked or discolored. Examples: aster yellows, mosaic virus, ringspot virus.

What to Do: Viral diseases in plants cannot be treated. Destroy infected plants; control disease spreaders such as aphids, leafhoppers and whiteflies.

WEEVILS
see Beetles

WHITEFLIES

Tiny, white, moth-like flying insects that flutter up into the air when the plant is disturbed. Live on undersides of leaves and suck juice out, causing yellowed foliage and weakened plants; deposit sticky honeydew, encouraging sooty mold.

What to Do: Try spray made from coffee grounds or garlic (see previous section). The most effective remedies are preventive. Remove infested plants so insects don't spread to rest of the garden. Destroy weeds where insects may live. Attract native predatory beetles and parasitic wasps with nectar plants such as yarrow. Spray severe cases with insecticidal soap. Use yellow sticky cards, available from local garden centers, or make your own sticky trap: mount tin can on stake, wrap can with yellow paper and cover with clear sandwich bag smeared with petroleum jelly; replace bag when full of flies. Plant sweet alyssum to repel whiteflies.

WILT

If watering hasn't helped a wilted plant, one of two wilt fungi may be at fault. *Fusarium wilt:* plant wilts, leaves turn yellow then die; symptoms generally appear first on one part of plant before spreading to other parts. *Verticillium wilt:* plant wilts; leaves curl up at edges, turn yellow then drop off; plant may die.

What to Do: Both wilts difficult to control. Choose resistant plant varieties; clean up debris at end of growing season. Destroy infected plants; solarize (sterilize) soil before replanting (contact your local garden center for assistance).

WORMS
see Caterpillars, Nematodes

ABOUT THIS GUIDE

The annuals in this book are organized alphabetically by their most familiar local common names. Additional common names and scientific names appear after the primary reference, and all names are in the index. The illustrated **Flowers at a Glance** section on pp. 5–9 will familiarize you with the different flowers quickly, and it will help you find a plant if you aren't sure what it's called.

Clearly indicated at the beginning of each entry are height and spread ranges, which encompass the measurements for all recommended species and varieties, along with the full range of flower colors for these plants. At the back of the book, the **Quick Reference Chart** summarizes different features and requirements of the annuals; you will find this chart handy when planning for diversity in your garden.

Each entry gives clear instructions and tips for seeding, planting and growing the annual, and it recommends some of our favorite species and varieties. Keep in mind that many more hybrids, cultivars and varieties are often available than we have space to mention. Check with your local greenhouses or garden centers when making your selection.

Pests or diseases that commonly affect an annual, if any, are also listed for each entry. Consult the 'Problems & Pests' section of the introduction for information on how to solve these problems.

Finally, we have kept jargon to a minimum, but check the glossary on p. 290 for any unfamiliar terms.

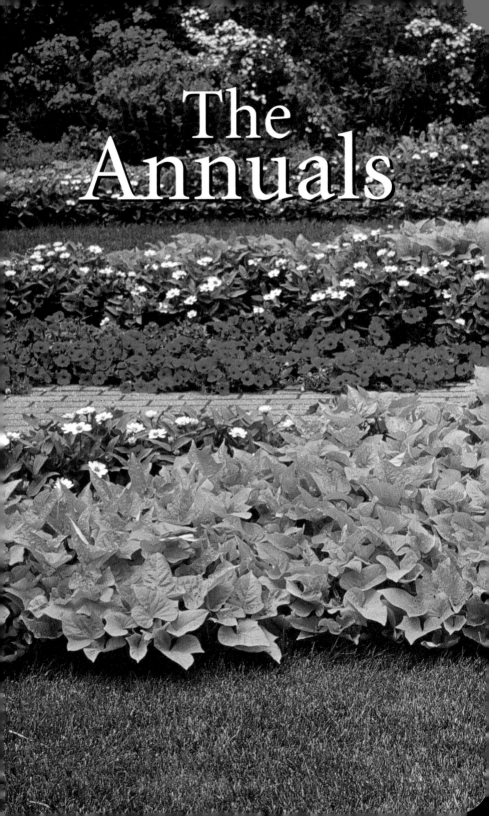

The
Annuals

African Daisy
Cape Daisy
Osteospermum

Height: 10–20" **Spread:** 10–20" **Flower color:** white, peach, orange, yellow, pink, lavender, purple; often with dark centers of blue-purple or other colors

AFRICAN DAISIES HAVE HAD THE REPUTATION OF FLOWERING poorly in hot weather, and of growing poorly if hit with heavy downpours or overhead watering. Fortunately, new varieties are appearing with increased heat and moisture tolerance. The crowning glory of these plants is the deep, rich flower eye surrounded by the bright daisy petals, often cupped and upward-facing. Look for the varieties with spoon-shaped petals if you are seeking something truly unique, although high night temperatures spoil the spoon shape. African daisies retain their good looks late into fall and can withstand temperatures as low as 25° F.

Planting

Seeding: Indoors in early spring

Planting out: Late April or May; plants can withstand light frosts if hardened off

Spacing: 12–18"

Growing

Plant in **full sun** in **light,** evenly **moist, moderately fertile, well-drained** soil. Do not overwater or let the plants wilt. Feed weekly with a well-balanced, water-soluble fertilizer that is high in nitrogen to keep them flowering all summer long. Use an organic mulch to cut down on the plants' water needs. Deadhead to encourage new growth and more flowers. Pinch young plants to encourage bushiness.

Tips

Osteospermum includes tender perennials and subshrubs from South Africa that we use as annuals. Recent breeding efforts have made African daisies much more likely to thrive in Midwest gardens. They are best used in containers or beds, and their daisy flowers look great mixed with plants such as petunia or verbena. When purchased in late summer, African daisies may flower into December in some downstate areas.

Recommended

O. ecklonis is a variable subshrub that can grow upright to almost prostrate. The species is almost never grown in favor of its wonderful cultivars. **Passion Mix** includes free-flowering, heat-tolerant plants growing 12" tall and 10" wide. The flowers come in pink, rose, purple and pure white,

Starwhirls Series (above),
Symphony Series 'Lemon' (below)

and have deep blue centers. This series was an All-America Selections winner in 1999. **Springstar Series** are compact, early-flowering plants that include the following five cultivars. 'Arctur' grows 14–16" tall and wide and produces white flowers. 'Aurora' grows 10–13" tall and wide and bears magenta to lavender flowers. 'Capella' is heat tolerant and grows 14–16" tall and wide. It produces large white flowers. 'Mira' grows 14–16" tall and wide and produces purple to deep magenta flowers with good heat tolerance. 'Sirius' bears magenta to deep red flowers with elongated petals. It grows 18–20" in height and spread. **Starwhirls Series** African daisies grow 12–18" tall and wide. They have unique spoon-shaped petals. Included in this series are 'Antaris,' which bears deep pink flowers, and 'Vega,' whose petals are white on the

Passion Mix (above),
Symphony Series 'Cream' & 'Orange' (below)

upper surface and dusky pink beneath.

O. **Symphony Series** from Proven Winners are mounding plants growing 10–15" tall and wide. They are very heat tolerant and flower well through the summer. '**Cream**' has cream flowers. '**Lemon**' has lemon yellow flowers. '**Orange**' grows slightly smaller and has wonderful tangerine orange flowers. '**Peach**' bears lightly flushed peachy pink flowers. '**Vanilla**' bears white flowers.

Problems & Pests

African daisies may experience problems with downy mildew, *Verticillium* wilt and aphids. Fungal diseases may occur in hot, rainy summers or if plants are overwatered.

O. ecklonis (above), Passion Mix (below)

You may find African daisies listed as either Osteospermum *or* Dimorphotheca. *The latter is a closely related genus that formerly included all the plants now listed as* Osteospermum.

Ageratum
Floss Flower
Ageratum

Height: 6–36" **Spread:** 6–18" **Flower color:** blue, purple, white, pink, burgundy

KNOWN FOR ITS TIGHT, BUTTON-LIKE BLOOMS, AGERATUM IS A natural for interplanting with silvery accents, playing off pinkish tones and complementing white flowers such as petunias. Blue is the most prevalent color for ageratum flowers, although reddish hues and some purples are available. The typical low, mounding varieties make good border plants, while the taller cultivars make a fine statement in a mixed border and are long-lasting cut flowers.

Planting

Seeding: Indoors in early spring, or direct sow after last frost. Don't cover the seeds, because they need light to germinate.

Planting out: Once soil has warmed

Spacing: About 4–12"

Growing

Ageratum prefers **full sun** but tolerates partial shade. The soil should be **fertile, moist** and **well drained**. This plant doesn't like to have its soil dry out; a moisture-retaining mulch will cut down on how frequently you have to water. Don't mulch too thickly or too close to the base of the plant, or it may develop crown rot or root rot. Adequate fertilization is required to keep ageratum blooming throughout the summer.

Though the plant needs deadheading to keep it flowering, the blossoms are extraordinarily long-lived, making ageratum an easy-care plant for sunny gardens. Removing the spent flowers will keep this plant looking good all summer.

'Shell Pink Hawaii' (above), 'Blue Hawaii' (below)

To dry ageratum flowers for crafts and floral arrangements, cut fresh flowers in the morning, bundle them together with rubber bands and hang them upside down in a location with good air circulation.

'Blue Horizon' (above), *A. houstonianum* (below)

Tips

The smaller varieties, which become almost completely covered with the fluffy flowerheads, make excellent edging plants for flowerbeds. They are also attractive grouped in masses or grown in planters. The taller varieties are useful in the center of a flowerbed and make interesting cut flowers.

Recommended

A. houstonianum forms a large, leggy mound up to 24" tall. Clusters of fuzzy blue, white or pink flowers are held above the foliage. Many cultivars are available; most have been developed to maintain a low, compact form that is more useful in the border. **Artist Hybrids** are compact, mounding plants 8–12" tall, with plentiful flowers. They have been bred to continue flowering throughout the summer, always overgrowing the old dead flowers with new blooms. 'Artist Alto Blue' grows 14–18" tall and 12–14" wide. It has the same excellent summer-long performance as the shorter Artist varieties. 'Artist Blue' has true blue flowers. 'Artist Purple' bears bright purple or plum-colored flowers. **'Bavaria'** grows about 10" tall, with blue and white bicolored flowers.

The genus name Ageratum *is derived from the Greek and means 'without age,' a reference to the long-lasting flowers. The specific* epithet houstonianum *refers not to the Texas city but to William Houston, who collected the flowers in Mexico and the Antilles.*

'Blue Hawaii' is a compact plant 6–12" tall, with blue flowers. 'Blue Horizon' is an upright cultivar with lavender blue flowers. It grows 24–36" tall. 'Leilani' ('Leilani Blue') is a vigorous, densely mounding plant growing 14–16" tall and 10–12" wide. It produces sky blue flowers. 'Red Sea' grows to 20" tall and bears burgundy red to wine red flowers. Pinching this cultivar encourages strong branching. 'Shell Pink Hawaii' has light pink double flowers on compact 6–12" tall plants.

Problems & Pests

Powdery mildew may become a problem. Be sure to plant ageratum in a location with good air circulation to help prevent fungal diseases.

'Blue Hawaii'

Agrostemma
Corn Cockle
Agrostemma

Height: 24–36" **Spread:** 12" **Flower color:** purple, pink, white

AGROSTEMMA IS KNOWN AS A FIELD WEED IN EUROPE, ESPECIALLY in corn crops, which explains the other common name of this plant. 'Cockle' is a name used to describe any of several weeds of grain and forage crops. This particular 'weed' finds its way into gardens by virtue of its silvery foliage and large, magenta, five-petaled, nearly flat flowers on solitary stems.

Planting

Seeding: Direct sow around last-frost date, or start indoors about a month earlier

Planting out: After last frost

Spacing: 8–12"

Growing

Agrostemma grows best in **full sun**. The soil should be of **poor fertility** and **well drained**. This plant prefers cool weather and may stop flowering during the hottest part of summer. Insert twiggy stakes around young plants to provide support as they grow. Deadhead to prolong the bloom and prevent self-seeding.

Tips

Agrostemma makes a good companion plant for bushy, silver-leaved perennials such as artemisia. The bright flowers stand out against the gray, and the stiffer perennial will support the weaker-stemmed annual. Agrostemma also makes a good filler plant for the middle of the border.

If you have a cutting garden, add agrostemma to the mix. Fresh cuts harvested just as the flowers open will last five days or more in a floral arrangement.

The seeds can cause stomachaches if ingested.

Recommended

A. githago is an upright plant 24–36" tall, with gray-green leaves and purple or white flowers. '**Milas**' ('Rose Queen') bears dark purple-pink flowers. '**Ocean Pearls**' ('Pearl') grows to 36" tall, producing silky white flowers with black flecks. '**Purple Foam**' produces lavender blooms and silver foliage.

Problems & Pests

Agrostemma may have rare problems with leaf spot.

A. githago

Agrostemma flowers attract butterflies to the garden. The nectar tube of the flower may be a little too deep for bees.

'Milas'

Amaranth

Amaranthus

Height: 3–5' **Spread:** 12–30" **Flower color:** red, yellow, green; flowers inconspicuous in some species grown for foliage

THESE STRAPPING PLANTS COME IN FOUR BASIC groups: the vegetable types that can be used like spinach as a salad or cooked vegetable ('Calaloo' is one variety if you can find it); the grain types (various species) whose seeds make a nutritious flour; the types grown for their intensely colorful foliage (*A. tricolor* and cultivars); and the love-lies-bleeding types that produce showy, rope-like flowerheads (*A. caudatus* and cultivars). And oh, yes, common pigweed is also an amaranth, so you know most amaranths will return next spring if their seed gets to your garden soil.

Several species of Amaranthus *are used as potherbs and vegetables because the leaves are high in protein.*

Planting

Seeding: Indoors about three weeks before last frost; direct sow once soil has warmed

Planting out: Once soil has warmed

Spacing: 12–24"

Growing

A location in **full sun** is preferable. The soil should be **poor to average** and **well drained**. Don't give these plants rich soil or overfertilize them, or their growth will be tall, soft and prone to falling over. Joseph's coat will also lose some of its leaf color when overfertilized; its colors are more brilliant in poorer soil.

Seeds started indoors should be planted in peat pots or pellets to avoid disturbing the roots when transplanting.

Tips

Love-lies-bleeding is attractive grouped in borders and in mixed

A. caudatus (photos this page)

'Viridis'

containers, where it requires very little care or water over summer.

Joseph's coat is a bright and striking plant that is best used as an annual specimen in a small group rather than in a large mass planting, where it quickly becomes overwhelming. It is also attractive mixed with large-leaved plants in the back of a border. It can self-sow in abundance, so remove unwanted seedlings in early summer to prevent them from overtaking the garden.

Recommended

A. caudatus (love-lies-bleeding) has erect stems and long, drooping, rope-like, fluffy red, yellow or green flower spikes that can be air dried. The plant grows 3–5' tall and 18–30" wide. **'Love-Lies-Bleeding'** has blood red flowers. **'Viridis'** has bright green flowers.

'Love-Lies-Bleeding'

Amaranth has astringent properties and is used by herbalists to stop bleeding and to treat diarrhea.

A. tricolor (Joseph's coat) is a bushy, upright plant with brightly colored foliage and inconspicuous flowers. It grows up to 5' tall and spreads 12–24". The foliage is variegated and can be green, red, bronze, chocolaty purple, orange, yellow or gold. '**Illumination**' has hanging foliage in crimson and gold. It grows 4' tall and 12" wide. '**Joseph's Coat**' has green, scarlet and cream foliage.

'Illumination' (above), 'Joseph's Coat' (below)

Problems & Pests

Cold nights below 50° F will cause leaf drop. Rust, leaf spot, root rot, aphids and some viral diseases are potential problems.

In ancient Greece, amaranth was regarded as a symbol of fidelity and immortality. The flowers were used to decorate tombs.

Angel's Trumpet
Datura, Trumpet Flower
Brugmansia, Datura

Height: 1–15' **Spread:** 1–6' **Flower color:** white, yellow, peach, purple

TWO DIFFERENT GROUPS
of plants go by the name angel's trumpet,
and they are commonly confused. The larger,
pendulous-flowered, tree-sized types with bright
green leaves are *Brugmansia*. They can grow
6–15' tall. Plants of this genus
are native to tropical
South and Central
America and rarely
set seed. The shorter, shrubby types with
upward-facing flowers, silvery green leaves
and thorny seedheads the size of golf balls
are *Datura*. Commonly called datura or
thorn apple, these plants range in height
from 12" to 36", depending on soil fertility.
Daturas are native to temperate regions and
can self-sow to return yearly, even in the
northern part of Illinois.

Planting

Seeding: Slow to germinate, and
may not grow to flowering size
until late summer. Start
indoors in mid-winter.

Planting out: Once soil
has warmed and frost
danger has passed

Spacing: 24–36"

Growing

All angel's trumpets prefer **full sun**. The soil should be **fertile, moist** and **well drained**. Don't allow plants to completely dry out, particularly during hot, dry weather. Plants recover quickly from wilting when watered.

Brugmansia really hates to dry out and thrives on very high fertility. Plant it in a large pot and feed weekly.

Propagate seeds indoors in early or mid-winter. Be patient because the seeds can be slow to germinate. Keep the soil moist but not soggy. The popularity of angel's trumpets has increased in recent years, and many garden centers carry started plants. Seeds can also be scattered outside in late April and will germinate on their own, blooming by early June. Cuttings taken in autumn will root quickly and can be overwintered in a sunny window. They'll be ready to plant outside early the next summer.

B. 'Charles Grimaldi' (above), *B. candida* (below)

Tips

Angel's trumpet flowers tend to open at night. Grow these plants where you will be able to enjoy their intoxicating scent in the evening—near a patio or in a large container on a deck. If angel's trumpets are planted under an open window, the scent will carry into the room. These plants are attractive used as specimens or in groups.

Brugmansia plants will become large quickly and create a tropical look on a patio or deck. Use a heavy pot because they easily become top-heavy and tip over.

D. metel 'Cornucopia' (above), *D. metel* (below)

Recommended

B. candida is a woody plant that can be grown in a bright room indoors in winter and moved outdoors in summer. In a container it rarely grows over 10'. Trim it back to keep it the size you want. It bears fragrant, white, trumpet-shaped flowers that may open only at night. '**Double Blackcurrant Swirl**' produces double lilac flowers with frilled margins. '**Ecuador**' bears double white flowers. '**Lemon Yellow**' produces an abundance of large, lemon yellow flowers. '**Shredded White**' bears unique double flowers with loosely bunched, white petals.

B. '**Charles Grimaldi**' is another woody plant. The large, funnel-shaped, pendulous flowers are a beautiful, luminous orange-yellow. This is an excellent container plant for a patio or deck. In a container it rarely grows over 10'.

B. '**Dr. Seuss**' ('Hetty Krauss') grows to about the same size as 'Charles Grimaldi.' The yellow-orange flowers are deeper yellow and have a wider flare. The American Brugmansia and Datura Society states that 'Dr. Seuss' is a parent of 'Charles Grimaldi.' 'Dr. Seuss' performs well in our northern climate.

B. '**Snowbank**' (variegated angel's trumpet) is a gorgeous new plant that grows 5' tall and 3–4' wide and produces large peach-colored flowers. The large leaves have a broad margin of ivory white with mid-green centers and pale to gray-green markings between the ivory white and mid-green.

D. x *hybrida* (*B.* x *hybrida*) includes several hybrid plants of uncertain parentage. **'Angel's Trumpets'** ('Angel') bears white flowers edged with pale pink. The hybrids in the **Queen Series** are commonly available, often offered in seed catalogs. 'Golden Queen' is a cultivar in this series that grows 3–4^1/$_2$' tall and bears yellow double flowers.

D. innoxia (*D. meteloides;* downy thorn apple) is a small tender perennial grown as an annual. It grows 36" tall and, if allowed, can sprawl to 5–6'. The flowers are white, pink or lavender. **Subsp.** *quinquecuspida* **'Missouri Marble'** grows 22" tall and 24" wide. The upright flowers are cream colored with wide flares tinged sky blue; they are attractive to butterflies.

D. metel (horn of plenty, jimsonweed, locoweed) is an annual that easily self-seeds. It grows to 12–36" tall and wide. The species produces single flowers, but many double- and even triple-flowered cultivars are available. **'Cornucopia'** has double purple and white flowers.

Problems & Pests

Problems with whiteflies, spider mites and mealybugs are possible, though more likely on plants grown indoors.

The American Brugmansia and Datura Society notes that the flower colors and forms of these plants can be affected by temperature, pH levels, nutrition, humidity, stress, sun and shade.

D. metel 'Cornucopia'

Angel's trumpets belong to the potato and tomato family, which also includes deadly nightshade. All parts of the plants, and especially the seeds, contain alkaloids that if ingested can cause liver damage, neurotoxicity and death. Avoid using these highly poisonous plants in places children frequent.

B. 'Charles Grimaldi'

Angel Wings

Summer Snapdragon, Brazilian Snapdragon
Angelonia

Height: 12–24" **Spread:** 12" **Flower color:** purple, blue, lavender, pink, white

ANGEL WINGS IS BENEFITING FROM a surge in interest from breeders who have introduced new series. The small blooms may remind you of snapdragons, orchids or angels. This is a lush plant with multiple blossoms in many blue, pink and white shades on each upright stem. And it loves the heat. If you like variegated flowers, try 'Purple Stripe' in the Angelmist Series (from Simply Beautiful) or 'Blue Bicolor' in the Angelface Series (from Proven Winners).

Planting

Seeding: Not recommended

Planting out: In warm soil after last frost

Spacing: 8–12"

Growing

Angel wings prefers **full sun** but tolerates a bit of shade. The soil should be **fertile, moist** and **well drained.** Though this plant grows naturally in damp areas, such as along ditches and near ponds, it is fairly drought tolerant.

This plant is not worth trying to save from year to year because it tends to lose its attractive habit as it matures. Cuttings can be taken in late summer and grown indoors over the winter to be used the following summer.

Tips

With its loose, airy spikes of orchid-like, lightly scented flowers, angel wings makes a welcome addition to the annual or mixed border. Include it in a planting at the side of a pond or stream or in a mixed planter. This plant makes a wonderful addition to container plantings, and it works well as a cut flower.

Recommended

A. angustifolia is a bushy, upright plant with loose spikes of flowers in varied shades of purple. '**Alba**' bears white flowers. Plants in the **Angelface Series** bear larger flowers and are more compact than the species, reaching 12–18" in height. In the series are 'Blue' with deep violet blue flowers, 'Blue Bicolor' with deep violet blue and white flowers and 'White' with white flowers. **Angelmist Series** are strong growers reaching 18–24" in height. They make fine cut flowers. This series includes 'Deep Plum,' 'Lavender,' 'Lavender Pink' and 'Purple Stripe,' with the flower colors their names suggest. '**Blue Pacific**' bears bicolored flowers of white and purple.

Problems & Pests

Aphids and powdery mildew can cause trouble.

The individual flowers look a bit like orchid blossoms, but angel wings is actually in the same family as snapdragons.

Angelmist Series (photos this page)

Baby's Breath
Gypsophila

Height: 12–36" **Spread:** 12–24" **Flower color:** white, pink, mauve

BABY'S BREATH, SHOWN HERE WITH 'STARGAZER' LILY, IS ONE OF the most familiar fillers in bouquets, and it can serve that same purpose in either garden beds or container plantings. Although some species can be found on the perennials bench at the garden center, these two annual species give longer-flowering shows. They allow gardeners an alternative to the usual planting of sweet alyssum for a small-flowering accent.

Planting

Seeding: Indoors in late winter; direct sow from mid-spring to early summer

Planting out: Mid-spring

Spacing: 8–18"

G. elegans (photos this page)

Growing

Baby's breath plants grow best in **full sun** but appreciate afternoon shade in southern regions of the state. The soil should be of **poor fertility,** and it should be **light, sandy** and **alkaline.** These plants are drought tolerant; take care not to overwater because they do not grow well in wet soil. Don't space the seedlings too far apart; slightly crowded plants flower more profusely.

Tips

The clouds of flowers are ideal for rock gardens, rock walls, mixed containers or borders with bold-colored flowers. Pinch back or shear occasionally to encourage reblooming. Baby's breath plants will reseed.

Recommended

G. elegans forms an upright 12–24" mound of airy stems, foliage and flowers. The flowers are usually white but may have pink or purple veining that gives the flowers a colored tinge. '**Carminea**' has deep carmine rose flowers. '**Covent Garden**' has very large, white flowers and grows to 20–36" tall. '**Red Cloud**' produces carmine to pink flowers in abundance. '**Rosea**' has pale rose pink flowers.

G. muralis is a smaller, more mounded species with dense, dark green foliage and flower clusters held above the foliage. It grows 12–18" tall and 12–20" wide and is a great filler in containers and baskets. '**Garden Bride**' bears double or semi-double pink flowers. This compact cultivar grows about 12" tall. '**Gypsy**' grows 12–14" tall and bears abundant semi-double to double pink flowers. '**Gypsy**' was an All-America Selections winner in 1997.

Problems & Pests

Most common problems are fungal diseases that can be avoided by not overwatering and not handling plants when they are wet. Leafhoppers can infect plants with aster yellows.

Gypsophila comes from the Greek words gypsos, *'gypsum' (sulfate of lime), and* philos, *'loving,' referring to the plants' preference for chalky, alkaline soils.*

Bachelor's Buttons
Cornflower
Centaurea

Height: 12–39" **Spread:** 6–24" **Flower color:** blue, violet, red, maroon, pink, white, yellow

THE ANNUAL VERSIONS OF *CENTAUREA* MAKE FINE ADDITIONS TO mixed borders and look good massed in sweeping plantings. The typically thistle-shaped flowers are best known for their perfectly clear blue color, but many other colors are now available. The upright form makes almost all varieties good cut flowers, and some are fragrant—try 'Sweet Sultan Dairymaid' and see if you think it smells like chocolate. Annual bachelor's buttons tend to self-seed, but typically seedlings will revert to the blue form even if you were initially growing another color.

Planting

Seeding: Direct sow in mid-spring or start indoors in late winter

Planting out: Around last frost

Spacing: 12"

The name bachelor's buttons arose in Victorian times, when these blossoms were worn as inexpensive boutonnieres. Today, a bachelor's button is a button attached with a wire, so it doesn't need to be sewn on.

Growing

Bachelor's buttons grow well in **full sun to partial shade** with afternoon shade. **Fertile, moist, well-drained** soil is preferable, but any soil is tolerated. Light frost won't harm these plants.

Seed started indoors should be planted in peat pots or pellets to avoid disturbing roots during transplanting. Shear spent flowers and old foliage in mid-summer for fresh new growth. Deadheading prolongs blooming.

C. cyanus (photos this page)

Tips

Bachelor's buttons are great filler plants in a mixed border or wildflower or cottage-style garden. Mix them with other plants—as the bachelor's buttons fade, the other plants can fill in the space they leave. They make good cut flowers and can also be dried. Try them in containers.

Recommended

C. cyanus is an upright annual that grows 12–36" tall and spreads 6–24". The flowers of this plant are most often blue but can be shades of red, pink, violet or white. **'Black Gem'** ('Black Ball,' 'Black Boy') has dark maroon, ruffled blooms above silvery foliage. It grows 18–30" tall. **Boy Series** plants grow up to 39" tall and have large double flowers in many colors. **Florence Series** includes compact, dwarf cultivars 12–18" tall, with flowers in various colors. **'Frosty Mixed'** grows 24–30" tall. It bears pastel flowers in blue, pink, rose, deep red and maroon, all edged with frosty white, or in white edged with pink. **'Polka Dot'** bears double flowers in

shades of blue, purple, red, pink and white on plants that grow about 12–20" tall.

C. imperialis **'Sweet Sultan Dairymaid'** (*Amberboa moschata* 'Dairy Maid,' *C. moschata* 'Dairy Maid') has bright yellow, 2" blooms on plants that grow 24" tall. The flower scent is said to resemble chocolate.

Problems & Pests

Aphids, downy mildew and powdery mildew may cause problems.

Bacopa
Sutera

Height: 2–12" **Spread:** 12–20" **Flower color:** white, lavender, lavender blue, rose, violet

IF YOU'VE NEVER BEEN SEDUCED INTO BRINGING HOME A BACOPA-draped hanging basket from a garden center in spring, you haven't shopped hard enough. Growers use cool spring temperatures and precise watering and fertilizing to produce stunning mounds of color. If only our summers were as accommodating. The jury is out on garden performance—potential ground-cover or burnout at the first sign of drought. Use bacopa in almost any container setting where you can keep even moisture and allow the trailing form to spill over an edge.

Planting

Seeding: Not recommended

Planting out: Once soil has warmed

Spacing: 12"

Growing

Bacopa grows well in **partial shade**, with protection from the hot afternoon sun. The soil should be of **average fertility, humus rich, moist** and **well drained**. Don't allow this plant to completely dry out, or the leaves and flowers will quickly die. Cutting back the dead growth may encourage new shoots to form.

Tips

Bacopa is a popular plant for hanging baskets, mixed containers and window boxes. Planting in a mixed container with impatiens works especially well, because the impatiens will act as a signal flag when the soil is dry.

Recommended

S. cordata is a compact, trailing plant 3–6" tall. It bears small, white flowers all summer. **Abunda Series** grows 2–4" tall and comes in blue, lavender and white varieties. **'Giant Snowflake'** is a vigorous grower with large white flowers. **'Glacier Blue'** grows 5–10" tall and produces soft, lavender blue flowers. **'Gold 'n' Pearls'** has gold-variegated foliage with white flowers. **Penny Candy Series** grows 12" tall and wide. Included in the series are 'Pink,' 'Rose' and 'Violet,' with flowers in colors of the same name.

Problems & Pests

Whiteflies and other small insects can become a real menace to this plant because the tiny leaves and dense growth make perfect hiding spots for them.

S. cordata cultivar

Bacopa is a perennial that is grown as an annual plant outdoors. It will thrive as a houseplant in a bright room.

'Giant Snowflake'

Begonia

Begonia

Height: 6–24" **Spread:** 6–24" **Flower color:** pink, white, red, yellow, orange, bicolored or picotee; plant also grown for foliage

VETERAN GARDENERS MAY OVERLOOK THE VENERABLE WAX begonias in favor of the more spectacular rexes or the more challenging tuberous begonias, but all deserve their spots in the garden. Wax begonias are tried and true, and few plants tolerate as wide a range of light. If you've never grown Dragon Wing, you have missed a great gardening joy. With its immense leaves and its blooms that last all summer, it makes a large container or a hanging basket something to remember.

Planting

Seeding: Indoors in early winter; seeds of wax begonias are tiny and can present a challenge for many gardeners

Planting out: Once soil has warmed

Spacing: According to spread of variety

Growing

Light or partial shade is best, although some of the wax begonias tolerate sun if their soil is kept moist. The soil should be **fertile,** rich in **organic matter, well drained** and **neutral to acidic.** Allow the soil to dry out slightly between waterings, particularly for tuberous begonias. Begonias like warm weather, so don't plant them before the soil warms in spring. If they sit in cold soil, they may become stunted.

Begonias can be tricky to grow from seed. The tiny seeds can be mixed with a small quantity of fine sand before sowing to ensure a more even distribution of seeds. Keep the soil surface moist but not soggy and do not cover the seeds. Maintain day-time temperatures at 70°–80° F and night temperatures above 50° F. Begonias can be potted individually once they have three or four leaves and are large enough to handle.

Tubers can be purchased in early spring and started indoors. Plant them with the concave side up. The tubers of tuberous begonias can also be uprooted when the foliage dies back and stored in slightly moistened peat moss over winter. The tubers will sprout new shoots in late winter

B. semperflorens

Begonias have attractive, colorful foliage. Use the dark-leaved forms of wax begonia for splashes of contrasting color next to a gray-leaved Helichrysum *or silver perennial* Lamium.

B. x *tuberhybrida* cultivars (above & opposite)

and can be potted for the following season.

Wax begonias can be dug out of the garden before the first frost and grown as houseplants in winter in a bright room.

Tips

All begonias are useful for shaded garden beds and planters. The trailing tuberous varieties can be used in hanging baskets and along rock walls where the flowers will cascade over the edges. Wax begonias have a neat rounded habit that makes them particularly attractive as edging plants. They can also be paired with roses and geraniums in a front-yard bed for a formal look. Creative gardeners are using the rex begonias, with their dramatic foliage, as specimen plants in containers and beds.

B. semperflorens (above),
B. x t. pendula (below)

Recommended

B. x *hybrida* **Dragon Wing** is a trade-name for a variety with deep scarlet to deep pink flowers and angel-winged foliage. This plant grows 12–15" tall and 15–18" wide, and it is heat tolerant.

B. **Rex Cultorum Hybrids** (rex begonias) are a group of plants developed from crosses between *B. rex* and other species. They grow 6–12" tall and 12–16" wide. Rex begonias are grown for their dramatic, colorful foliage and are especially stunning used amongst hostas in the shade garden. The **Great American Cities Series** from Proven Winners has wild, dark color combinations including the following selections. 'Chicago Fire' foliage features magenta centers deepening to near-black edges. 'Denver Lace' has pointed silver, pink, purple and green leaves. 'Maui Mist' has dark pink foliage sprinkled with silver. 'New York Swirl' produces large leaves with silvery pink centers and margins and purple veins.

B. x *tuberhybrida* cultivar

Wax begonias are ideal flowers for lazy gardeners because they are generally pest free and bloom all summer, even without deadheading.

B. semperflorens cultivar

B. semperflorens (wax begonias) have pink, white, red or bicolored flowers and green, bronze, reddish or white-variegated foliage. The plants are 6–14" tall and 6–24" wide. Plants in the **Ambassador Series** are heat tolerant and have dark green leaves and white, pink or red flowers. **Cocktail Series** plants are sun and heat tolerant. They have bronzed leaves and red, pink or white flowers. **Harmony Series** grow 6–8" tall and 8–10" wide. Plants in this companion series to Prelude Series have bronze foliage and pink, scarlet or white flowers. **Maestro Series** are 6–12" tall with green and bronze foliage and white, pink and red flowers. **Prelude Series** reach 6–8" in height and 8–10" in spread and have green foliage with coral, pink, scarlet, rose, white or bicolored flowers. 'Queen Red' is a vigorous grower bearing fully double, rose-like, red flowers. **Senator Series** begonias are very similar to the Ambassador Series but with bronze foliage. Plants in the **Victory Series** grow 8–10" tall

B. x t. pendula (above),
B. semperflorens & *Ageratum* (below)

with green or bronze foliage. The flowers come in pink or red shades and can also be white or bicolored.

B. x *tuberhybrida* (tuberous begonias) are generally sold as tubers. The flowers come in many shades of red, pink, yellow, orange or white. They can also be picotee, with the petal margins colored differently than the rest of the petal. The plants grow 8–24" tall and wide. **Charisma Series** plants tolerate heat and rain and grow 12" tall and wide. They produce $2^1/_2$" wide, double flowers in pink, salmon orange, scarlet or deep rose. **Non-stop Series** begonias can be started from seed. They grow about 12" tall and wide; their double and semi-double flowers come in pink, yellow, orange, red or white. *B.* x *t. pendula* includes attractive pendulous begonias with flowers in many bright shades. **Illumination Series** is a cascading type of *B.* x *t. pendula* for baskets and other container plantings. Different varieties have flowers in white, salmon, apricot, scarlet or rose on plants 18–20" tall.

Problems & Pests

Problems with stem rot and gray mold can result from overwatering.

Rex begonias can also be grown as houseplants, and in that form the leaves take on different colors depending on the levels of light.

Rex hybrid 'New York Swirl' (above), *B.* x *hybrida* Dragon Wing (below)

Bidens

Bidens

Height: 10–24" **Spread:** 12–24" or more **Flower color:** yellow

BIDENS IS VERY POPULAR IN EUROPEAN WINDOW BOXES. WITH ITS daisy-like yellow blossoms, lacy foliage and trailing habit, bidens is a wonderful choice for container and basket plantings. In a cottage garden, this fragrant, sprawling plant makes a good filler. It is especially stunning combined with red geraniums.

This cheerful plant in the daisy family is constantly in flower and makes a wonderful annual groundcover.

Planting

Seeding: Direct sow in late spring or start indoors in late winter

Planting out: After last frost

Spacing: 12–24"

Growing

Bidens grows well in **full sun**. The soil should be **average to fertile, moist** and **well drained.**

If plants become lank and unruly in summer, shear them back lightly to encourage new growth.

Tips

This species of *Bidens* is native to the southern U.S. and Mexico, so it is well equipped to handle full sun and heat in your garden. It can be included in mixed borders, containers, hanging baskets and window boxes. Its fine foliage and attractive flowers make it useful for filling spaces between other plants.

Recommended

B. ferulifolia (B. aurea) is a bushy, mounding plant 12–24" tall, with ferny foliage and bright yellow flowers. 'Golden Goddess' has even narrower leaves and larger flowers. 'Goldie' grows only 10–12" tall and bears bright yellow, sweetly scented flowers. 'Peter's Gold Carpet' grows 10–15" tall and has large, fragrant, golden yellow flowers.

Problems & Pests

Problems can occur with fungal diseases such as leaf spot, powdery mildew and rust.

B. ferulifolia

Bidens is also known by the names bur marigold, beggar-ticks and bootjacks, all referring to the two-pronged fruits that easily stick to clothing and fur.

B. ferulifolia & Calibrachoa 'Terra Cotta'

Black-Eyed Susan
Coneflower, Gloriosa Daisy
Rudbeckia

Height: 8–36" or more **Spread:** 12–20" **Flower color:** yellow, orange, red, brown or sometimes bicolored; brown or green centers

PERENNIAL *RUDBECKIAS* HAVE SO TAKEN OVER THE IMAGINATION of American gardeners that *R. hirta* cultivars have been overlooked. That situation is slowly changing, however, as breeders develop plants such as 'Indian Summer,' 'Cherokee Sunset' and 'Prairie Sun,' all of which have been named All-America Selections in recent years. These cultivars have bright new colors and different heights than the traditional species. They are so special you will itch to move them out of a naturalistic garden to a cottage or more formal planting.

Planting

Seeding: Indoors in late winter; direct sow in mid-spring

Planting out: Late spring

Spacing: 18"

Growing

Black-eyed Susan grows equally well in **full sun** or **partial shade**. The soil should be of **average fertility, humus rich, moist** and **well drained**. This plant tolerates heavy clay soil and hot weather. If it is growing in loose, moist soil, Black-eyed Susan may reseed itself. Keep cutting the flowers to promote more blooming.

'Prairie Sun' (above), 'Becky' (below)

Tips

Black-eyed Susan can be planted individually or in groups. Use it in beds and borders, large containers, meadow plantings and wildflower gardens. This plant will bloom well even in the hottest part of the garden. It also makes a long-lasting vase flower.

R. hirta is a perennial that is grown as an annual. It is not worth trying to keep over winter because it grows and flowers quickly from seed.

Recommended

R. hirta forms a bristly mound of foliage 12–36" tall and 12–18" wide. It bears bright yellow, daisy-like flowers with brown centers in summer and fall. **'Becky'** is a dwarf cultivar up to 12" tall, with large flowers in solid and mixed shades of yellow, orange, red and brown. **'Cherokee Sunset'** bears 3–4$\frac{1}{2}$" semi-double and double flowers in yellow, orange, brown and red. **'Indian Summer'** has huge flowers 6–10" across, on sturdy stems 36"

tall or taller. **'Irish Eyes'** grows up to 30" tall and has green-centered single flowers. **'Prairie Sun'** grows 36" tall and 20" wide. Its yellow flowers are 4" in diameter and have distinctive green centers. **'Toto'** is a dwarf cultivar that grows 8–18" tall, small enough for planters.

Problems & Pests

Good air circulation will help prevent fungal diseases such as powdery mildew, downy mildew and rust. Aphids can also cause problems occasionally.

Black-Eyed Susan Vine
Thunbergia

Height: 5' or more **Spread:** equal to height, if trained **Flower color:** yellow, orange, violet blue or white, usually with dark centers

DUAL USAGE IS A GREAT ATTRIBUTE IN A PLANT, AND BLACK-EYED Susan vines qualify. They can cascade earthward from a hanging basket, or twine their way upward from a planting in a pot or garden bed. It is the distinctive dark eye of the flower that gives rise to the common name. This plant is not related to the other black-eyed Susan *(Rudbeckia)*.

Planting

Seeding: Indoors in mid-winter; direct sow in mid-spring

Planting out: Late spring

Spacing: 12–18"

Growing

Black-eyed Susan vines grow well in **full sun, partial shade** or **light shade.** Grow in **fertile, moist, well-drained** soil that is high in **organic matter.** Make sure to keep the soil evenly moist.

Tips

Black-eyed Susan vines can be trained to twine up and around fences, walls, trees and shrubs. They are also attractive trailing down from the top of a rock garden or rock wall or growing in mixed containers and hanging baskets.

These vines are perennials treated as annuals. They can be quite vigorous and may need to be trimmed back from time to time, particularly if they are brought inside for winter. To acclimatize the plants to the lower light levels indoors, gradually move them to more shaded locations. Keep in a bright room out of direct sunlight for winter. The following spring, harden off the plants before moving them outdoors.

Recommended

T. alata is a vigorous, twining climber with yellow flowers. 'Alba' has white flowers. The commonly available **Susie Series** bear large flowers in yellow, orange or white.

T. grandiflora (skyflower, sky vine, blue trumpet vine, clock vine) is also a twining climber but bears stunning, pale violet blue flowers. It takes far longer to come into flower than does *T. alata*—look for the 3" blooms in late summer or fall.

T. alata cultivar

Fashion wire frames into any shape to grow your vine into whimsical topiary. Black-eyed Susan vines also make excellent hanging plants. The blooms are trumpet shaped, with the dark centers forming a tube.

T. alata

Blanket Flower

Gaillardia

Height: 12–24" **Spread:** 12–24" **Flower color:** red, orange or yellow, often in combination

FOR ALL THE COLORFUL PUNCH THAT *GAILLARDIA*S BRING TO A planting, the perennial version often looks weedy by late summer and tends to find its way to places in the garden where it was not meant to be. The annual versions pack even more color, especially the double-flowering cultivars that have earned All-America Selections status. 'Red Plume' and 'Sundance Bicolor' are AAS winners, and both are easy-care additions to any garden bed.

Both the annual and the perennial Gaillardia species are known for their plentiful, fire-bright blooms.

Planting

Seeding: Indoors in late winter; direct sow in mid-spring

Planting out: Mid- to late spring

Spacing: 12"

Growing

Blanket flower prefers **full sun.** The soil should be of **poor or average fertility, light, sandy** and **well drained.** The less water this plant receives, the better it will do. Don't cover the seeds; they need light to germinate. They also require warm soil.

Deadhead to encourage more blooms and to discourage fungal disease in humid weather.

'Red Plume' (above), 'Sundance Bicolor' (below)

Tips

Blanket flower has an informal, sprawling habit that makes it a perfect addition to a casual cottage garden or mixed border. Because it is drought tolerant, it is well suited to exposed, sunny slopes, where it can help retain soil until more permanent plants have grown in.

Recommended

G. pulchella grows 12–24" tall and wide and forms a basal rosette of hairy leaves. The daisy-like flowers are red with yellow tips. **Plume Series** has double flowerheads in vibrant shades of red or yellow and includes the popular cultivar 'Red Plume.' This dwarf plant grows about 12" tall, with an equal spread, and blooms for a long time. **'Sundance Bicolor'** grows 16" tall and wide and has globe-shaped flowers of deep mahogany red with yellow. Its sprawling habit lends it to container and basket uses.

Problems & Pests

Possible problems include leafhoppers, powdery mildew, aster yellows, rust and bacterial and fungal leaf spot. If you avoid overwatering, most problems will not become serious.

Blood Flower

Asclepias

Height: 24–36" **Spread:** 24" **Flower color:** orange-red, yellow

I FIRST BOUGHT THIS PLANT BECAUSE ITS SCIENTIFIC NAME WAS SO lyrical. It outperformed its name by light-years, sending up vivid red-orange flowers that make its perennial counterparts appear washed out and inconsequential. Like its relatives, the annual species forms long seedpods that split open, revealing silky hairs and tiny black seeds. The native *Asclepias* species, better known as milkweeds or butterfly weeds, are major food sources for monarch butterflies, who also lay their eggs on the stems and leaves.

Planting

Seeding: Indoors in late winter; soil temperature about 62° F

Planting out: Once frost danger has passed and soil has warmed

Spacing: 18–24"

Growing

Blood flower prefers to grow in **full sun** and a **well-drained, moderately fertile to infertile** soil. This plant is very drought resistant.

In its native habitat, *A. curassavica* is considered to be a bit weedy because it readily self-sows. In a Zone 5 winter, the seed may not survive, but it will make it through a warmer Zone 6 winter.

Tips

This striking plant makes an interesting accent in the center of a border. If grown in containers, it can be moved indoors for the winter.

If overwintering this plant, give it a very bright location and a large space to grow in. Otherwise it will become stressed and more susceptible to pests and diseases.

Recommended

A. curassavica is a shrubby, upright, evergreen South American subshrub that we treat as an annual in our climate. It forms a clump of upright leafy stems with clusters of red, orange or yellow flowers. '**Silky Gold**' has golden yellow flowers. '**Silky Scarlet**' has flowers with bright red undersides and orange hoods; it is good for attracting bees.

Problems & Pests

Blood flower can experience problems with aphids and mealybugs. Whiteflies may be a problem if the plant is grown indoors.

A. curassavica (photos this page)

The genus Asclepias *is named for Asklepios, the Greek god of medicine, and refers to the reputed healing properties of these plants.*

Blue Throatwort

Trachelium

Height: 18–36" **Spread:** 12–30" **Flower color:** blue, violet blue, reddish violet

BLUE FLOWER LOVERS CAN NEVER HAVE TOO MANY CHOICES, especially for cut-flower arrangements. This plant provides a welcome way to beat the blues and add that sought-after color to bouquets and beds. The 1/4" wide flowers are borne in clusters that give the plant an airy appearance, making blue throatwort appropriate as a filler in both mixed borders and bouquets.

Blue throatwort is a source of nectar for butterflies.

Planting

Seeding: Indoors in early spring or direct sow after last frost

Planting out: After last frost

Spacing: 12"

Growing

Blue throatwort grows well in **full sun to partial shade.** In the hottest summers, this plant appreciates a location with shelter from the midday sun. The soil should be **moderately fertile, well drained** and **moist** but not overly wet. Blue throatwort can tolerate dry soil and competition from tree roots.

Tips

This plant will do well in the middle or back of an annual or mixed bed. It makes a great addition to the cut-flower garden.

Recommended

T. caeruleum is an erect perennial that is grown in Illinois as an annual. It grows 24–36" tall and 18–30" wide. Cloudy sprays of small, tubular to star-shaped, blue to violet blue, lightly fragrant flowers appear over a long period in summer on long, red-tinged flower stalks. **Devotion Series** plants grow 18–30" tall in the garden and around 12" tall when grown in pots or containers. Cultivars to look for in this series include 'Blue Improved,' 'Burgundy,' 'Purple Improved' and 'White Improved.' These cultivars flower early and will grow to a very uniform height. '**Lake Superior**' bears reddish violet flowers all summer.

T. caeruleum (above), Devotion Series (below)

Problems & Pests

Blue throatwort is generally problem free but may have some trouble with aphids and spider mites.

Browallia
Amethyst Flower
Browallia

Height: 6–18" **Spread:** up to 8–18" **Flower color:** purple, blue, white

ALTHOUGH THE SPECIES IS AN UPRIGHT PLANT, BREEDING has brought about a cascading habit that makes browallia a good choice for hanging baskets and other containers where blue color combinations are desired. A new variety, 'Jingle Bells Mix,' has colors of lavender, indigo and powder blue as well as white. Browallia can be brought inside and used as a houseplant after the garden season.

Browallia was named by the great botanist Linnaeus for his contemporary John Browall (1707–55), a Swedish bishop and botanist.

Planting

Seeding: Indoors in late winter

Planting out: Once soil has warmed

Spacing: 8–10"

Growing

Browallia tolerates any light conditions from **full sun to full shade,** but flower production and color are best in partial shade. The soil should be **fertile** and **well drained.** Do not cover the seeds when you plant them because they need light to germinate. They do not like the cold, so wait several weeks after the last frost before setting out the plants. Pinch tips often to encourage new growth and more blooms.

Cultivar (above), *B. speciosa* (below)

Tips

Grow browallia in mixed borders, mixed containers or hanging baskets.

Browallia can be brought indoors at the end of the season to be used as a houseplant during winter. It can also be grown as a houseplant all year long.

Recommended

B. speciosa forms a bushy mound of foliage. This plant grows 8–18" tall, with an equal or narrower spread, and bears white, blue or purple flowers all summer. **'Garden Leader Blue'** has deep blue flowers on plants that grow 6–12" tall and 10–14" wide. **Jingle Bells Hybrids** include 'Blue Bells,' 'Jingle Bells Mix' and 'Silver Bells,' which vary from 8" to 12" in both height and spread.

Problems & Pests

Browallia is generally problem free. Whiteflies may cause some trouble.

Caladium

Caladium

Height: 18–24" **Spread:** 18–24" **Flower color:** greenish white; plants grown for foliage

SHADE IS A CROSS THAT MANY OF US BEAR, AND USUALLY NOT cheerfully. 'More color!' is the refrain heard over and over when discussing shade. With all the focus on flowers, many gardeners forget about the absolute riot of colors that the foliage of caladium brings. The striking leaf venation of this plant enhances the smashing leaf colors. If you are searching for bold texture in the shade garden, caladium is a must.

Planting

Seeding: Not recommended; grow from tubers

Planting out: After danger of frost has passed and soil has warmed

Spacing: 18–24"

Growing

Caladium prefers **partial to full shade** and **moist, well-drained, humus-rich, slightly acidic** soil.

Start the tubers inside in soil-less planting mix, with the soil temperature at a minimum of 70° F. Once the new plants have leafed out, they can handle cooler soil temperatures of minimum 55° F. When planting out, add a little bonemeal or fishmeal to the planting hole. Make sure the knobby side of the tuber is facing up and is level with the soil surface or just under.

Dig the tubers in fall after the leaves die back. Remove as much soil as possible and let the tubers dry for a few days. Store tubers in slightly damp peat moss at 55°–60° F. Tubers can be divided in spring before planting. These divisions can be susceptible to fungal diseases owing to their freshly exposed surfaces.

Tips

Caladium is an excellent plant for providing a tropical feel to your garden. It does very well around water features and in woodland gardens. It is equally effective in the herbaceous border in a mass or as a specimen, and it makes a great container plant.

When growing caladium in a container, there is no need to dig the tubers in fall. Simply bring the whole container inside for the winter.

Recommended

C. x *hortulanum* (elephant's ears, heart-of-Jesus, mother-in-law plant, angel's wings) is a complex group of hybrids with *C. bicolor* as the main parent. The often tufted, narrow to wide, arrow-shaped leaves are dark green and variously marked with red, white, pink, green, rose, salmon, silver or bronze. Each leaf can grow 6–14" long.

The garden caladiums come in two main forms. Most common are the fancy-leaved hybrids, which have *C. marmoratum* and *C. bicolor* as parents. *C. bicolor* has large, green-margined red leaves. *C. marmoratum* has green leaves variously marked with gray, greenish white, yellow-green and silver. Strap-leaved selections, with *C. picturanum* as one of the parents, have narrower leaves than the fancy-leaved types. *C. picturanum* has narrow, strap-like leaves. Some of the *C.* x *hortulanum* hybrids have all three species in their ancestry. All of these plants are native to woodland edges in tropical South America.

Do not confuse Caladium bicolor *with its cousin* Colocasia esculenta, *the taro root. The two have similarly shaped leaves, and both grow well in partial shade. The leaves of* Colocasia, *however, come in only one color—green.*

Problems & Pests

Slugs, snails, tuber rot, bacterial and fungal leaf spots and root-knot nematodes are possible problems. Caladium may also have occasional trouble with aphids and spider mites.

Like other members of the arum family, all parts of caladium contain tiny bundles of sharp crystals that may irritate the skin. Ingesting the plant causes painful burning and swelling of the mouth and throat.

Calendula
Pot Marigold, English Marigold
Calendula

Height: 10–24" **Spread:** 8–20" **Flower color:** cream, yellow, gold, orange, apricot

EASILY AT HOME IN THE CUT-FLOWER OR HERB GARDEN, OR AS AN adornment in the vegetable patch, calendula's sunny yellow countenance shines throughout the entire growing season. Calendula petals are used in salads and soups, and the herbal lore of this plant stretches back to the days of the ancient Romans. In the garden, calendula prefers the cooler days of spring and fall, so a sequential planting of these easy-care flowers should take care of their disdain for mid-summer heat.

Calendula flowers are popular kitchen herbs that can be added to stews for color or salads for flavoring. They can also be brewed into a healing infusion that is useful as a wash for cuts and bruises.

Planting

Seeding: Direct sow in mid-spring; sow indoors a month or so earlier

Planting out: Mid-spring

Spacing: 8–10"

Growing

Calendula does equally well in **full sun** or **partial shade**. It likes cool weather and can withstand a light frost. The soil should be of **average fertility** and **well drained**. Young plants are sometimes hard to find in nurseries because calendula is quick and easy to start from seed and that is how most gardeners grow it. A second sowing in mid-summer gives a good fall display. Deadhead to prolong blooming and keep plants neat.

Tips

This informal plant looks attractive in borders and mixed into the vegetable patch. It can also be used in mixed planters. Calendula is a cold-hardy annual and often continues flowering until the ground freezes completely.

Recommended

C. officinalis is a vigorous, tough, upright plant 12–24" tall, with a slightly lesser spread. It bears daisy-like, orange to yellow, single flowers. Cultivars can have single or double flowers in a wide range of yellow and orange shades. **'Bon Bon'** is a dwarf plant that grows 10–12" tall and comes in all available colors. **'Fiesta Gitana'** ('Gypsy Festival') is a dwarf plant that bears flowers in a wide range of colors. **'Pacific Beauty'** is a larger plant, growing about 18" tall.

Double-flowered cultivar (above), *C. officinalis* (below)

It bears large flowers in varied colors. **'Pink Surprise'** bears pale orange and apricot flowers tinged with pink.

Problems & Pests

Calendula plants are often trouble free, but they can have problems with aphids and whiteflies as well as powdery mildew and fungal leaf spot. They usually continue to perform well even when they are afflicted with such problems.

Calibrachoa

Calibrachoa

Height: 6–12" **Spread:** up to 24" **Flower color:** pink, purple, yellow, reddish orange, red, white, blue

NO, THEY'RE NOT STARVED PETUNIAS, BUT A GENUS ALL THEIR own. Calibrachoa hybrids have hit the market running because they are so floriferous. These low-growing, compact, vigorous plants tolerate our summer heat and require no deadheading, as the plants are self-cleaning. They are great to use as groundcovers or in containers and hanging baskets. Feed your calibrachoa often, especially when it is in containers and baskets.

Calibrachoa flowers close at night and on cloudy days.

Planting

Seeding: Propagate from cuttings; cannot be grown from seed

Planting out: After last frost; plants are also frost tolerant if hardened off

Spacing: 6–15"

Growing

Calibrachoa needs **full sun** for peak flowering but can tolerate some shade. The soil should be **fertile, moist** and **well drained**. Though it prefers to be watered regularly, calibrachoa is fairly drought resistant once established. It will bloom well into fall; the flowers become hardier as the weather cools and may survive temperatures down to 20° F.

Tips

Popular for planters and hanging baskets, calibrachoa is also attractive in beds and borders. This plant grows all summer and needs plenty of room to spread or it will overtake other flowers. Pinch the flowers back to keep your calibrachoa compact. In a hanging basket, it will produce plentiful bell-shaped blooms.

Recommended

Calibrachoa hybrids have a dense, trailing habit. They bear small, colorful, petunia-like flowers all summer. **Lirica Showers Series** includes low-growing plants whose varieties bear white, yellow, blue, pink or rose flowers. **Million Bells Series** includes 'Cherry Pink' with reddish pink flowers on upright plants; 'Terra Cotta' with yellow, orange or brick red flowers and an upright habit; 'Trailing Blue' with dark blue or purple, yellow-centered flowers;

'Terra Cotta' (above),
Million Bells Series with *Heliotropium* (below)

'Trailing Pink' with pink, yellow-centered flowers; and 'Yellow' with bright yellow flowers. Plants in the **Superbells Series** are more heat tolerant and vigorous and have larger flowers than any previous series. Included in this semi-trailing series are 'Blue,' 'Coral Pink,' 'Pink,' 'Red,' and 'White.'

Problems & Pests

Wet weather and cloudy days may cause leaf spot and delayed blooming. Watch for slugs, which like to chew on the petals.

Canterbury Bells
Cup-and-Saucer Plant
Campanula

Height: 18–36" **Spread:** 12" **Flower color:** blue, purple, pink, white

IF PLANTED OUT IN FALL, CANTERBURY bells will flower the following spring. If you seed it in spring, accept a lesser flower quality the first season and prepare for a better show in the following spring. This old-fashioned flower is known as Canterbury bells if the blooms are single, and as cup-and-saucer plant if the blooms are double.

Planting

Seeding: Indoors in mid-winter

Planting out: Early spring

Spacing: 6–12"

Growing

Canterbury bells prefers **full sun** but will tolerate partial shade. The soil should be **fertile, moist** and **well drained**. This plant will not suffer if the weather cools or if there is a light frost.

When sowing, leave seeds uncovered because they require light for germination. Harden off in a cold frame or on a sheltered porch before planting out. Canterbury bells transplants easily, even when in full bloom.

C. medium (photos this page)

Tips

Planted in small groups, Canterbury bells looks lovely in a border or rock garden. It also makes a good addition to a cottage garden or other informal garden where its habit of self-seeding can keep it popping up year after year. The tallest varieties produce good flowers for cutting. Use dwarf varieties in planters.

Canterbury bells is actually a biennial treated as an annual. This is why the plants must be started so early in the year. Small plants, those purchased in 3½" pots, are usually too small to grow to flowering size the first year.

Recommended

C. medium forms a basal rosette of foliage. The pink, blue, white or purple cup-shaped flowers are borne on tall spikes. The species grows 24–36" high and spreads about 12". '**Bells of Holland**' is a dwarf cultivar about 18" tall. It has flowers in various colors. '**Champion**' is a true annual cultivar, flowering much sooner from seed than the species or many other cultivars. Blue or pink flowers are available. '**Russian Pink**' is an heirloom plant that was recently reintroduced. It is another true annual cultivar that bears light pink flowers.

Problems & Pests

Occasional, but infrequent, problems with aphids, crown rot, leaf spot, powdery mildew and rust are possible.

Cockscomb
Celosia, Woolflower
Celosia

Height: 10"–4' **Spread:** usually equal to height **Flower color:** red, orange, gold, yellow, pink, purple

AS A FIRST-TIME COCKSCOMB GROWER, I CHOSE A VARIETY THAT became a showstopper: three-plus feet tall with cockscombs 8" or 9" across, blood red on blood red stems, with deep red foliage. People would knock on the door to ask what the plant was. Alas, after several years of searching for a similar variety, I gave up. The plume types seemed to be more popular, and now the feather and wheat types of *C. spicata* are gaining well-deserved popularity. But if you've never grown a true cockscomb, give it a shot— you'll love the novelty of the amazing flowerhead.

Planting

Seeding: Indoors in late winter; direct sow in mid- to late spring in southern Illinois

Planting out: Once soil has warmed

Spacing: According to spread of variety

Growing

A **sheltered** spot in **full sun** is best. The soil should be **fertile** and **well drained,** with plenty of **organic matter** worked in. Cockscombs like to be watered regularly.

It is preferable to start cockscombs directly in the garden. If you need to start them indoors, start the seeds in peat pots or pellets and plant them into the garden before they begin to flower. If left too long in pots, cockscombs will suffer stunted growth and won't be able to adapt to the garden. Keep seeds moist while they are germinating and do not cover them.

Use the expected spread of the variety to determine the appropriate spacing. It will usually be between 6" and 18".

Tips

Cockscombs work well in borders and beds as well as planters. The flowers make interesting additions to arrangements, either fresh or dried.

A mass planting of plume celosia looks bright and cheerful in the garden. The popular crested varieties work well as accents and as cut flowers.

Recommended

C. argentea is the species from which both the crested and plume-type cultivars have been developed. The species itself is never grown. **Cristata Group** (crested celosia) has the blooms that resemble brains or rooster combs. This group has many

C. spicata 'Startrek' (above),
C. argentea Plumosa Group (below)

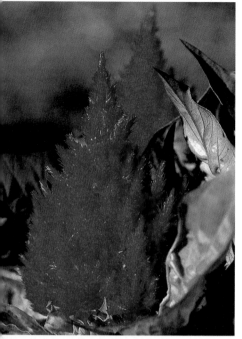

C. argentea Plumosa Group (above),
Cristata Group (below)

varieties and cultivars. 'Brain Mix Tall' grows 3–4' tall and has flowers in several colors. 'Fireglow' has brilliant red combs 6" across on plants 12–18" tall. 'Jewel Box' bears flowers in red, pink, orange, yellow and gold on compact plants 10" tall. **Plumosa Group** (plume celosia) has feathery, plume-like blooms. This group also has many varieties and cultivars. 'Century' has neat, much-branched plants up to 24" tall and 18" in spread, with flowers in many bright colors. 'Fairy Fountains' is a compact plant, 12" tall, that bears long-lasting flowers in red, yellow and pink.

C. spicata (*C. argentea* Spicata Group; wheat celosia) grows 10–18" tall and produces spike-like clusters of pink to rose flowers, often with a metallic sheen. **'Flamingo Feather'** grows 24–36" tall and has slender spikes of pink to white flowers. **'Flamingo Purple'** is bushier and taller with purple to white flower spikes and dark red-green stems and leaves. It grows about 36" tall. Another interesting recent development from the species is **'Startrek,'** which has bright pink flowers that radiate out from a central spike.

To dry the colorful plumes, pick the flowers when they are at their peak and hang them upside down in a cool, shaded place.

Problems & Pests

Cockscombs may develop root rot if planted out too early or if over-watered when first planted. Cool, wet weather is the biggest problem.

The genus name Celosia *is derived from the Greek* keleos, *'burning,' referring to the intensely colorful blooms.*

C. argentea Cristata Group (above), Plumosa Group (below)

Coleus

Solenostemon (Coleus)

Height: 6–36" or more **Spread:** usually equal to height **Flower color:** light purple; plant grown for multi-colored foliage

COLEUS WAS TRADITIONALLY THE STALWART OF SHADE GARDENS. The problem was the colors—the pastels could look washed out and the leaf shapes were not as interesting as those of some other shade plants. Enter the Ducksfoot Series, with their unique foliage, and the many other varieties with improved, sensational colors. Some new varieties actually do better in sun than shade. One of the small-leaved varieties grew an interesting stem some years ago, and the sport was taken as a cutting and grown at Cantigny Gardens in Wheaton. 'Cantigny Royale' is now available in some garden centers. Try it—it's either a dark, luminous purple or, in some cases, light brown.

Planting

Seeding: Indoors in winter

Planting out: Once soil has warmed

Spacing: 12"

Growing

Seed-grown coleus prefers to grow in **light or partial shade,** but it tolerates full shade if the shade isn't too dense and full sun if the plants are watered regularly. Cultivars propagated from cuttings thrive in **full sun to partial shade.** The soil for all coleus should be of **high to average fertility, humus rich, moist** and **well drained.**

'Life Lime'

Coleus can be trained to grow into a standard (tree) form by pinching off the side branches as they grow. Once the plant reaches the desired height, pinch from the top.

Place the seeds in a refrigerator for one or two days before planting them on the soil surface. Low temperatures will assist in breaking their dormancy. They need light to germinate. Seedlings will be green at first, but leaf variegation will develop as the plants mature. As your seedlings develop, decide which ones you like best, and when they are about three pairs of leaves high, pinch off the tip. The plants will begin to branch out. Repeated pinching will create a very bushy plant.

Coleus is easy to propagate from stem cuttings, and in doing so you can ensure that you have a group of plants with the same leaf markings, shapes or colors. The cuttings should be about three leaf pairs long. Make the cut just below a leaf pair, and then remove the two bottom leaves. Plant the cuttings in pots filled with a soil mix intended for starting seeds. Keep the soil moist but not soggy. The plants should develop roots within a couple of weeks.

Tips

The bold, colorful foliage creates a dramatic display in beds and borders. Coleus can also be used in mixed containers and as an edging plant. It can be grown indoors as a houseplant in a bright room.

Pinch off flower buds when they develop, because the plants tend to stretch out and become less attractive after they flower.

Recommended

S. scutellarioides (*Coleus blumei* var. *verschaffeltii*) forms a bushy mound of foliage. The leaf edges range from slightly toothed to very ruffled. The leaves are usually multi-colored with shades ranging from pale greenish yellow to deep purple-black. The size may be 6–36", depending on the cultivar, and the spread is usually equal to the height. Hundreds of cultivars are available. Plants in the **Dragon Series** have bright yellow-green margins around variably colored leaves. **Ducksfoot Series** are fully sun-tolerant plants with flat leaves that rather resemble duck feet. This series includes 'Ducksfoot Red' with glowing burgundy foliage; 'Indian Frills' with purple- and pink-tinged green foliage; 'Midnight' with very dark purple to black foliage; and 'Super Ducksfoot' with large, burgundy-specked yellow and rose leaves. **'Garnet Robe'** has a cascading habit and dark wine red leaves edged with yellow-green. **'Molten Lava'** bears foliage with burgundy red centers and flaming red, lightly scalloped margins.

'Palisandra' features velvety, purple-black foliage. 'Scarlet Poncho' has wine red leaves edged with chartreuse. **Wizard Series** includes compact plants with heart-shaped leaves.

Sun-loving varieties grown from cuttings include '**Alabama Sunset**' with spectacular orange, red and yellow leaves; '**Dark Star**' with dark, rich purple-black, scalloped leaves; '**Kingswood Torch**' with large, lovely, rich red leaves edged in dark purple; and '**Life Lime**,' a large, gold-leaved variety with occasional splashes of maroon.

Problems & Pests

Mealybugs, scale insects, aphids and whiteflies can cause occasional trouble.

Although coleus is a member of the mint family, with the characteristic square stems, it lacks the enjoyable culinary or aromatic qualities.

Coreopsis
Coreopsis

Height: 18"–4' **Spread:** up to 18" **Flower color:** yellow, red, orange, brown

THESE ANNUAL RELATIVES OF THE POPULAR PERENNIAL COREOPSIS bring warm and sunny hues to naturalized plantings with their bright, daisy-like, 2$^1/_2$" wide blooms. Coreopsis should be deadheaded to keep the plants neat in more formal plantings. In a wildflower garden, however, they can be left to their own devices. These cheerful annuals may persist in the garden for a few seasons as they reseed, but they are often crowded out in a naturalized setting by vigorous perennials.

Planting
Seeding: Indoors in mid-winter; direct sow after last frost

Planting out: After last frost

Spacing: 8–12"

Growing

Coreopsis plants prefer **full sun**. The soil should be of **average to high fertility, light** and **well drained**. Poor soil is also tolerated but with somewhat reduced flowering. Good drainage is the most important factor for these drought-tolerant plants.

Tips

C. *grandiflora* 'Early Sunrise' (above),
C. *tinctoria* (below)

These annuals look comfortable growing in front of a rustic wooden fence or repeating in clusters in a bed of perennials. They make a beautiful color combination planted with deep purple *Heuchera* or royal purple *Heliotropium*. Well suited to naturalized meadow plantings, coreopsis can also be used in informal beds and borders, where they will flower all season if deadheaded regularly. These plants also make lovely cut flowers.

Coreopsis plants can be blown over or have their stems broken during heavy rain or high winds. Twiggy branches, inserted while the plants are small, will give the plants a support structure to grow up into. In very windy spots, it is best to use the dwarf forms of coreopsis.

Recommended

C. grandiflora forms a clump of stems and foliage. It grows 18–36" tall, spreads about 18" and bears bright yellow single flowers all summer. '**Early Sunrise**,' an All-America Selections winner, bears bright yellow double flowers on compact plants about 18" tall.

C. tinctoria forms a clump of basal leaves and tall, branching stems with just a few leaves. It grows up to 4' tall and spreads up to 18". The flowers are usually bright yellow with dark red bands at the petal bases; flowers in red, orange or brown are also possible. '**Mardi Gras**' blooms in a range of yellows, reds and bicolors on plants 18–24" tall.

Problems & Pests

Slugs, snails and fungal diseases can be problems.

Cosmos

Cosmos

Height: 1–7' **Spread:** 12–18" **Flower color:** magenta, pink, purple, white, yellow, gold, orange, red, scarlet, maroon

COSMOS HAVE REACHED AN EXALTED STATUS IN AMERICAN horticulture: no self-respecting annual garden is without them. These easy-care, colorful, lacy plants can be included in almost any type of bedding plan. The colors are plentiful, and a new cultivar, *C. sulphureus* 'Polidor,' bears semi-double blooms in warm hues. One species even has flowers alleged to smell like chocolate. All cosmos attract birds and butterflies, and most bring a star quality to the cut-flower bouquet.

Planting

Seeding: Indoors in late winter; direct sow after soil has warmed

Planting out: After last frost

Spacing: 12–18"

Growing

Cosmos like to grow in **full sun**. The soil should be of **poor or average fertility** and **well drained**. Cosmos are drought tolerant. Overfertilizing and overwatering can reduce the number of flowers produced. Yellow cosmos will do better if sowed directly in the garden.

Keep faded blooms cut to encourage more buds. Cosmos will often reseed themselves if a few flowers are left on the plants to produce the seeds.

Although these plants may need staking, they are difficult to stake. Save yourself the trouble of staking by planting cosmos in a sheltered location or against a fence. Alternatively, grow shorter varieties. If staking can't be avoided, push twiggy branches into the ground when the plants are young and allow them to grow up between the branches for support. The branches will be hidden by the mature plants.

C. bipinnatus (above) & with *Godetia* (below)

The name Cosmos *is from the Greek* kosmos, *meaning 'good order' or 'harmony.'*

C. atrosanguineus (above), *C. bipinnatus* (below)

Tips

Cosmos are attractive in cottage gardens, at the back of a border or mass planted into an informal bed or border. Their cut flowers make lovely, long-lasting fillers in fresh arrangements.

Recommended

C. atrosanguineus (chocolate cosmos) has recently become popular among annual connoisseurs for its fragrant, deep maroon flowers that some claim smell like chocolate. The plant is upright, growing to 30" tall, but tends to flop over a bit when the stem gets too long.

C. bipinnatus (annual cosmos) has many cultivars. The flowers come in magenta, rose, pink or white, usually with yellow centers. Old varieties grow 3–6' tall, while some of the newer cultivars grow 12–36" tall. **'Daydream'** has white flowers flushed with pink at the petal bases. It grows up to 5' tall. **'Psyche Mixed'** grows 3–4' tall and bears large, showy, semi-double flowers in deep lavender pink, magenta rose, white and red. **'Sea Shells'** has flowers in all colors and petals that are rolled into tubes. It grows up to 42" tall. **'Sensation'** bears large white or pink flowers and grows up to 4' tall. **Sonata Series** includes compact plants up to 24" tall that bear red, pink or white flowers.

C. sulphureus (yellow cosmos) has pale yellow, gold, orange or pale yellow-red flowers. Old varieties grow 7' tall, and new varieties grow 1–4' tall. **'Bright Lights'** grows 3–4' tall and has semi-double, red- to orange-yellow flowers. **'Cosmic Orange'** and

'Cosmic Yellow' are stockier plants with coarser foliage, growing 12–18" tall with orange and yellow flowers respectively. **Ladybird Series** includes compact dwarf plants, 12–14" tall, that rarely need staking. The foliage is not as feathered as in other cultivars. 'Polidor' grows 18–24" tall and bears $2^{1}/_{2}$" wide, semi-double flowers in shades of orange, yellow and red.

Problems & Pests

Cosmos rarely have any problems, but watch for wilt, aster yellows, powdery mildew and aphids.

C. sulphureus (above)

C. bipinnatus

Creeping Zinnia
Sanvitalia

Height: 3–8" **Spread:** 12–18" **Flower color:** yellow or orange with dark brown, green or purple centers

SPREADING PLANTS ARE USEFUL FOR FILLING IN GAPS, EITHER in garden beds or in containers. Creeping zinnia works well as a filler plant because its growth habit and small flowers will not overgrow or outshine its showier neighbors. If your creeping zinnia suffers in the mid-summer heat, be patient; cooler weather usually encourages a second flush of blooms.

Planting

Seeding: Indoors in mid- to late winter; direct sow in mid-spring

Planting out: After last frost

Spacing: 12"

Growing

Creeping zinnia prefers **full sun**. The soil should be of **average fertility, light, sandy** and **well drained**.

Do not cover the seeds when you sow them because they need light to germinate. Seeds started indoors should be planted in peat pots or pellets to avoid disturbing the roots when transplanting.

Tips

Use creeping zinnia as an annual groundcover or edging plant. It also looks dramatic in hanging baskets and in mixed containers.

Creeping zinnia is one of the easiest annuals to grow. It is also one of the easiest to damage with too much care; overwatering and overfertilizing can quickly kill it.

Recommended

S. procumbens forms a low mat of foliage up to 8" tall and 18" wide. Small yellow or orange, daisy-like flowers with dark centers are borne from summer until long into fall. 'Cuzco Yellow' is a larger-flowered new variety that produces lemon yellow blooms with lime green centers. It is a strong grower that trails vigorously out of a pot. 'Gold Braid' grows 3–6" tall, spreads 12–18" and bears yellow-orange blooms with dark centers. 'Irish Eyes' also grows 3–6" tall and 12–18" wide. It bears orange flowers with green centers. 'Mandarin Orange,' an All-America Selections winner, has bright orange flowers with black centers. 'Sunbini' is a very compact grower with dark green leaves and green-centered gold

S. procumbens (photos this page)

flowers. 'Yellow Carpet' is a low-growing dwarf variety that is up to 4" tall and 18" wide. It has bright yellow flowers with dark centers.

Problems & Pests

Do not overwater your creeping zinnia, or it will suffer mildew and other fungal problems.

Cup Flower

Nierembergia

Height: 6–12" **Spread:** 6–12" **Flower color:** blue, purple or white, with yellow or blue centers

THE FLOWERS OF *NIEREMBERGIA* FLOAT LIKE STARS ATOP FERN-LIKE foliage. The low habit of these plants makes them suitable for rock gardens as well as a variety of container options such as window boxes. Although cup flowers can handle drought in the garden, they need to be kept moist and fed in container situations.

Planting

Seeding: Indoors in mid-winter

Planting out: Spring

Spacing: 6–12"

Growing

Cup flowers grow well in **full sun** or **partial shade**. The soil should be of **average fertility, moist** and **well drained**. Fertilize little, if at all, except when growing these plants in containers.

Tips

Use cup flowers as annual groundcovers. They are also useful for bed and border edges, rock gardens, rock walls, containers and hanging baskets. These plants grow best when summers are cool, and they can withstand a light frost.

Recommended

N. 'Blue Eyes' is a new, slightly larger-growing cultivar (at the high end of the height range). It has lacy leaves and large white flowers with blue, star-shaped eyes. It loves heat and humidity and works well as a mid-range plant in a container or as a mid-border plant.

N. caerulea (N. hippomanica) forms a small mound of foliage. This plant bears delicate, cup-shaped flowers in lavender blue with yellow centers. '**Mont Blanc**' is an All-America Selections winner that bears white flowers with yellow centers.

N. frutescens 'Purple Robe' is a dense, compact plant producing deep purple flowers with golden eyes.

Problems & Pests

Slugs are likely to be the worst problem for these plants. Because cup flowers are susceptible to tobacco mosaic virus, don't plant them near any tomatoes or flowering tobaccos.

N. caerulea 'Mont Blanc' (photos this page)

Cup flowers belong to the highly poisonous nightshade family, so be sure to keep them away from children and pets.

Cuphea

Cuphea

Height: 6–24" **Spread:** 10–36" **Flower color:** red, pink, purple, violet, green, white

A MEXICAN HEATHER *(C. HYSSOPIFOLIA),* OR TWO OR THREE, came home with me from a garden center one spring, bursting with bluish purple flowers and not a tag in the pot. A subsequent visit to the garden center unmasked the identity of the plant, which had already made a lasting impression. Although cupheas are a novelty in many garden centers, it is likely that with a little marketing, the colorful common names alone—cigar flower, firecracker plant, tiny mice, batface—will move them off the shelves.

Planting

Seeding: Sow seed indoors in early spring, approximately 8–10 weeks before last-frost date

Planting out: After risk of frost has passed

Spacing: 10–24"

Growing

Cupheas prefer **full sun to partial shade** in **moderately fertile, well-drained** soil. They do best if given regular water but can handle short periods of drought. Batface cuphea, in particular, can really take the heat.

Tips

Cupheas are excellent ornamentals for containers of all descriptions. The container can be brought into the house for the winter and kept in a sunny window. They are also effective in the annual or mixed border and as edging plants.

Recommended

C. hybrida **'Purple Trailing'** is a vigorous grower reaching 6–12" in height and 10–14" in spread. Its lavender blooms and dark green foliage work well in hanging baskets and mixed containers.

C. hyssopifolia (Mexican heather, false heather, elfin herb) is a bushy, much-branched plant that forms a flat-topped mound 12–24" tall, with a spread slightly greater than the height. The flowers have green calyces (sepal rings) and light purple, pink or sometimes white petals. The plants bloom from summer to frost. **'Allyson Purple'** ('Allyson') reaches only 6–12" in height and

C. llavea 'Batface' (above),
C. ignea (below)

bears lavender flowers. 'Desert Snow' features white flowers.

C. ignea (*C. platycentra;* cigar flower, firecracker plant) is a spreading, freely branching plant 12–24" tall and 12–36" wide. The common names were inspired by the thin, tubular, bright red flowers that are borne freely from late spring to frost. This species can also be used as a houseplant.

C. llavea (batface cuphea, St. Peter plant, tiny mice) is a mounding to spreading plant 12–18" tall and 12–24" wide. It produces an abundance of flowers with green to violet calyces (sepal rings) and bright red petals. The two longest stamens are bearded purple, giving the flower the appearance of a colorful bat or mouse face. '**Batface**' grows 6–12" tall and has a purple 'face' with red 'ears.'

C. llavea 'Batface' (above),
C. ignea (below)

C. x *purpurea* is a hybrid that was the result of crossing *C. llavea* and *C. procumbens*. 'Firecracker Red Hood' grows 10–14" tall. It has tubular flowers with purple ribs and protruding red petals. 'Firefly' has magenta red flowers. 'Summer Medley' is a neat, mounding plant 12–18" tall, with violet and red flowers.

Problems & Pests

Cupheas may experience problems with whiteflies, aphids, root rot, powdery mildew and leaf spot.

The genus name Cuphea *arises from the Greek word* kyphos, *'curved,' referring to the curved seed capsules.*

C. *ignea* (above),
C. *hyssopifolia* (below)

Dahlberg Daisy
Golden Fleece
Thymophylla

Height: 6–12" **Spread:** 12" **Flower color:** yellow; less commonly orange

HERE'S ONE DAISY THAT IS COMPACT ENOUGH TO BE USED IN containers and even hanging baskets. The leaves have a light scent. Floriferous during cool weather, this plant may revive in autumn if deadheaded during the summer. This is one of a number of annuals that can be grown to look attractive on a garden center bench—just in time for spring sales. If it doesn't last all summer, don't blame your brown thumb.

This cheerful annual rarely suffers from pest or disease problems.

Planting

Seeding: Indoors in mid-winter; direct sow in spring

Planting out: After last frost

Spacing: 8–12"

Growing

Plant Dahlberg daisy in **full sun**. Any **well-drained** soil is suitable, although soil of **poor or average fertility** is preferred. Dahlberg daisy prefers cool summers. In hot climates, it flowers in spring.

Direct-sowed plants may not flower until quite late in summer. For earlier blooms, start the seeds indoors. Don't cover the seeds, because they require light to germinate. Dahlberg daisy may self-sow and reappear each year.

Trimming your plants back when flowering seems to be slowing will encourage new growth and more blooms, particularly when the weather cools.

Tips

This attractive plant can be used along the edges of borders, along the tops of rock walls, or in hanging baskets or mixed containers. In any location where it can cascade over and trail down an edge, Dahlberg daisy will look wonderful.

Recommended

T. tenuiloba (*Dyssodia tenuiloba*) forms a mound of ferny foliage. From spring until the summer heat causes it to fade, it produces many bright yellow, daisy-like flowers.

Dahlberg daisy has fragrant foliage that some people compare to a lemon-thyme scent; perhaps this is the origin of the name Thymophylla, *'thyme-leaf.'*

Dahlia

Dahlia

Height: 8"–5' **Spread:** 8–18" **Flower color:** purple, pink, white, yellow, orange, red, bicolored

DAHLIAS HAVE BEEN TAGGED THE ULTIMATE 'MAN'S FLOWER' because of the mostly male growers who compete to show the best and largest dahlia. Attend a dahlia show, and you may hear about how these aficionados put up shade cloths to let just the right amount of light in, pinch out side shoots to force energy into one bloom and calculate the exact number of days it takes for a bloom to fully open before a show. If you'd rather be spared these details, simply enjoy the immense variety of dahlia colors and shapes on display. These plants prefer cooler conditions, so late-summer and autumn days bring out the best show of color.

Planting

Seeding: Indoors in mid- to late winter; direct sow in spring

Planting out: After last frost

Spacing: 12"

Growing

Dahlias prefer **full sun**. The soil should be **fertile,** rich in **organic matter, moist** and **well drained.** Dahlias are tuberous perennials that are treated as annuals. Tubers can be purchased and started early indoors. The tubers can also be lifted in fall and stored over winter in slightly moist peat moss. Pot them and keep them in a bright room when they start sprouting in mid- to late winter.

If there is a particular size, color or form of dahlia that you want, it is best to start it from tubers of that type. Seed-grown dahlias show a great deal of variation in color and form because the seed is generally sold in mixed packages.

In the 18th century, the first European breeders of these Mexican plants were more interested in them as a possible food source. The blooms were thought to be unexceptional.

To keep dahlias blooming and attractive, it is essential to remove the spent blooms.

Tips

Dahlias make attractive, colorful additions to a mixed border. The smaller varieties make good edging plants and the larger ones make good replacement plants for shrubs. Varieties with unusual or interesting flowers can be grown as attractive specimen plants.

Recommended

Of the many dahlia hybrids, which range in height from 8" to 5', most must be grown from tubers. Some dahlias can be started from seed with good results.

Seed-started dahlias include *D.* **'Figaro,'** which forms a round, compact plant 12–16" tall. The flowers are small and double or semi-double, in a wide variety of colors. The plants grow and flower quickly and look very good grouped in a border or in

Mixed cutting bed

containers. *D.* 'Harlequin' forms a compact plant that flowers quickly from seed. Flowers are solid or bicolored, single or semi-double, in many shades. Many hybrid seeds are sold in mixed packets based on flower shape, such as collarette, decorative or peony-flowered. Tubers of specific types and colors can be purchased in late winter and early spring.

Problems & Pests

The most likely problems a dahlia grower may encounter are aphids, powdery mildew and slugs. If a worse problem afflicts your dahlias, it may be best to destroy the infected plants and start over.

Dahlia flowers are categorized by size, from giants more than 10" in diameter to mignons up to 2" in diameter. They are also categorized by flower type—for example, peony, formal and informal decorative, semi-cactus and waterlily.

Dahlia cultivars span a vast array of colors, sizes and flower forms, but breeders have yet to develop true blue, scented and frost-hardy varieties.

Informal decorative type

Semi-cactus type

Formal decorative type

Peony type

Diascia
Twinspur
Diascia

Height: 7–16" **Spread:** 20" **Flower color:** shades of pink

ONE CAN NEVER HAVE ENOUGH SHOWY, ABUNDANTLY FLOWERING container plants, and diascias qualify mightily for this role. The plants are usually less than a foot tall and drape beautifully over a pot or basket rim. The most intriguing feature of the flower is the protruding lower petal that seems to catch light and bring one's eye right into the cup-shaped bloom. Diascia flower colors are bright and clean—the corals and apricots especially so.

Planting

Seeding: Indoors in spring

Planting out: After the last frost

Spacing: 18"

Growing

Diascias prefer **full sun**. The soil should be **fertile, moist** and **well drained**. When hardened off, diascias withstand frosts and can be planted out in early April. They generally bloom well into fall.

Many of the older diascia varieties don't thrive in the high humidity and heat of our summers, but newer varieties have been bred to take the heat and still flower wonderfully throughout the summer. Plants whose flowers fade during the hottest part of summer will revive and bloom again as temperatures drop in fall.

Deadheading and regular weekly applications of a water-soluble fertilizer will help keep blooms coming all summer. If flowering becomes sparse in searing summer heat, shear to encourage a fresh flush of blooms in a few weeks when the weather becomes cooler.

'Red Ace' (above), 'Strawberry Sundae' (below)

Diascias are native to the mountains of South Africa and are related to penstemons, snapdragons and foxgloves.

'Coral Belle' (above), *D. barberae* (below)

Tips

Diascias are perennials treated as annuals. They are attractive in a rock garden or mass planted in a border. They are very nice in hanging baskets and containers when planted at the edge and allowed to cascade over and soften the side of the pot. Pinch plant tips to increase bushiness.

Recommended

D. barberae is a low-growing plant that bears loose spikes of pink flowers from mid-summer to frost. **'Blackthorn Apricot'** has apricot-colored flowers and flowerheads that point downwards. **'Pink Queen'** has light, shimmery pink flowers on long, slender stalks.

D. **Flying Colors Series** from Proven Winners includes plants that grow 8–12" tall, are very heat and frost tolerant and have large, early-blooming flowers. **'Apricot'** has lovely apricot flowers and dense, dark green foliage. **'Coral'** has bright coral flowers. **'Trailing Antique Rose'** has a trailing habit and bears deep rose flowers.

D. **'Little Charmer'** grows 7–10" tall and features medium to bright pink flowers and plentiful foliage. It has excellent heat tolerance.

D. **'Red Ace'** is a trailing, vigorous grower reaching 10–14" in height. The flowers are a very deep rose pink and abundant. It is a heat-tolerant selection.

D. **'Strawberry Sundae'** grows 7–10" tall with trailing stems and bright pink flowers. It does well in both the summer heat and the cooler spring and fall.

D. Summer Celebration Series,
from Proven Selections, includes
great performers in the heat of summer and in the cooler spring and
fall. The series boasts abundant
flowers and dense, compact foliage
on plants 10–16" tall. **'Coral Belle'**
is a quick-growing hybrid that
forms a dense mound of bright
green foliage. This variety is said to
be the most heat tolerant of all the
diascias. The flowers are a delicate
coral pink. **'Ice Pole'** bears bright
white flowers that really stand out
against the foliage.

'Strawberry Sundae' (above), 'Little Charmer' (below)

D. Whisper Series from Simply
Beautiful includes semi-trailing,
spreading plants 10–15" tall.
'Cranberry Red' has dark, burgundy
flowers. The series also includes
'Apricot,' 'Lavender Pink' and
'Salmon Red,' bearing flowers in
the colors their names suggest.

Problems & Pests

Watch out for slugs.

The genus name Diascia *comes
from the Greek words* di *or* dis,
'two,' and askos, *'sac,' referring to
the two spurs each flower possesses.
The alternative common name
twinspur is a rough English
translation of the genus name,
and it is a very accurate
description of the flowers.*

Dusty Miller

Senecio

Height: 12–24" **Spread:** equal to height or slightly narrower
Flower color: yellow or white; plant grown for silvery foliage

NOVICE GARDENERS MAY VIEW THIS PLANT AS THE 'SOMETHING different' in their flowerbeds. It's a lovely companion plant, and it is easy to grow and care for. More experienced gardeners are aware of other annuals and perennials that bring the same contrasting silver-foliage element to the garden, some with more interesting textures, flowers and forms. Nevertheless, dusty miller is a standard must-use plant in beds of colorful flowers. It can be effectively worked into containers and arrangements as well.

Planting

Seeding: Indoors in mid-winter

Planting out: Spring

Spacing: 12"

Growing

Dusty miller prefers **full sun** but tolerates light shade. The soil should be of **average fertility** and **well drained**.

Tips

The soft, silvery, lacy leaves of this plant are its main feature, and it is used primarily as an edging plant. It is also used in beds, borders and containers. The silvery foliage makes a good backdrop to show off the brightly colored flowers of other plants.

Pinch off the flowers before they bloom. They aren't showy and steal energy that would otherwise go to the foliage.

Recommended

S. cineraria forms a mound of fuzzy, silvery gray, lobed or finely divided leaves. Many cultivars have been developed with impressive foliage colors and shapes. **'Cirrus'** has lobed, silvery green or white foliage. **'Silver Dust'** has deeply lobed, silvery white foliage. **'Silver Lace'** has delicate, silvery white foliage that glows in the moonlight.

Mix dusty miller with geraniums, begonias or cockscombs to really bring out the vibrant colors of those flowers.

'Cirrus' (photos this page)

Fan Flower

Scaevola

Height: up to 8" **Spread:** 12–36" or more **Flower color:** blue, purple, white

FAN FLOWER MAY BE A COLORFUL COMMON NAME FOR THIS interesting plant, but I like the genus name even more. *Scaevola* comes from a Latin word that means 'left-handed,' referring to the asymmetrical distribution of all five petals on one side of the flower. We lefties have to stick together. This plant isn't exactly a prima donna, but it does best with a regimen of consistent moisture and relatively frequent feeding with a balanced fertilizer that includes micronutrients and iron.

Regular pinching and trimming will keep your fan flower bushy and blooming.

Planting

Seeding: Indoors in late winter

Planting out: After last frost

Spacing: 1–4'

Growing

Fan flower grows well in **full sun** or **light shade**. The soil should be of **average fertility, moist** and **well drained**. Water regularly, because this plant doesn't like to dry out completely. It does, however, recover quickly from wilting when watered.

Tips

Fan flower is popular for hanging baskets and containers, but it can also be used along the tops of rock walls and in rock gardens where it can trail down. This plant makes an interesting addition to mixed borders or can be used under shrubs, where the long, trailing stems will form an attractive groundcover.

Recommended

S. aemula forms a mound of foliage from which trailing stems emerge. The fan-shaped flowers come in shades of purple, usually with white bases. The species is rarely grown because there are many improved cultivars. '**Blue Shamrock**' can eventually spread 36" wide or more. It has deep blue flowers. '**New Wonder**' is an award-winning plant with blue flowers and a low-growing habit. '**Saphira**' is a new compact variety with deep blue flowers. It spreads about 12". '**Sun Fan**' is an especially sun-tolerant selection with smaller and lighter blue flowers than the others. '**Zigzag**' is a well-branched,

S. aemula cultivar

Given the right conditions, this Australian plant will flower abundantly from April through to frost.

vigorous grower. The flowers have white petals, each with a lilac blue stripe up the middle.

Problems & Pests

Whiteflies may cause problems for fan flower if the plant becomes stressed from lack of water.

Flowering Maple
Chinese Lantern
Abutilon

Height: 3–24" **Spread:** 12–24" or more **Flower color:** red, pink, white, orange, yellow

THE STANDARD RAP AGAINST FLOWERING MAPLES IS THAT THE very striking flowers face downward, making them less than impressive in a bedding situation. Newer cultivars, including Bella Mix from Ball Seed Company in West Chicago, have wheel-shaped, dappled flowers that face both outward and upward on compact plants. Try them as flowering houseplants, a niche they have occupied for many years. High light and low night temperatures seem to be the key to keeping a new flower opening virtually every day.

Planting

Seeding: Indoors in early winter with soil at 70°–75° F; blooms in 5–6 months from seed

Planting out: After last frost

Spacing: 24"

Growing

Flowering maples grow well in **full sun** but can benefit from some shade during the afternoon. The soil should be **average to fertile, moist** and **well drained**. Pinch back growing tips to encourage bushy growth.

Tips

Include flowering maples in borders and mixed containers. Container-grown plants are easier to bring indoors for the winter. There they will continue to bloom for most of the fall and winter. Indoor plants need a bright window and should be kept well watered in summer and just moist in winter.

Recommended

A. x *hybridum (A. globosum)* is a bushy, mound-forming shrub 12–24" wide that can be treated as an annual or wintered indoors and moved outside for the summer. Drooping, cup- or trumpet-shaped flowers are borne for most of the summer. Named varieties are available, but most seed catalogs sell seeds in mixed packets, so flower colors will be a surprise. **Bella Mix** from Ball Seed grows only 14–16" tall and bears large flowers in pastel shades of yellow, ivory, pink, rose, coral red, apricot and peach. **'Crimson Belle'** has deep red flowers.

A. megapotamicum

Flowering maples are among the few plants that, depending on the climate, may be grown as annuals, perennials or shrubs.

A. x hybridum

'**Mobile Pink**' is lower growing and spreads more than the species. It has gray-tinted green foliage and salmon pink flowers with a reddish calyx (ring of sepals). '**Roseus**' has pale pink flowers with darker pink veins. '**Vesuvius Red**' has very bright, fiery red flowers.

A. megapotamicum (trailing abutilon) grows about 3–6" tall and 12–18" wide with arching stems and bright green foliage. Large red calyces (sepal rings) surround small yellow flowers with protruding purple stamens. '**Variegatum**' has strongly yellow-blotched foliage.

A. pictum (A. striatum) grows 12–24" tall and wide. The flowers have orange-yellow petals with red veins and protruding stamens. '**Thompsonii**' has peach flowers with darker orange veins and heavily yellow-blotched foliage.

A. x *hybridum* (photos this page)

A. '**Savitzii**' is a compact, bushy plant generally growing to 12–18" tall and wide, but it may reach 24" in height and spread. It produces gray-tinted, heavily cream-marbled green foliage. It occasionally bears salmon flowers but is best used as a foliage plant.

Problems & Pests

Few problems affect flowering maples in the garden, but whiteflies, mealybugs and scale insects can cause trouble when plants are moved indoors.

A. x hybridum (photos this page)

These plants are in the mallow family and are not related to maples, as the common name suggests.

Flowering Tobacco

Nicotiana

Height: 6"–5' **Spread:** 10–24" **Flower color:** red, pink, green, yellow, white or purple

WITH SO MANY VARIETIES OF FLOWERING TOBACCO TO CHOOSE from, a gardener must assess priorities: is it more important to have stronger plants in more vivid colors, or to have blooms with a strong evening fragrance? The tall species of *Nicotiana* are justifiably famous for their aroma but have some disadvantages: the plants are tall and may need staking; some flowers close during the heat of the day, opening only morning and evening; and the coarse habit is a bit like that of their infamous cousin—the one with the big bold leaves first made famous in colonial times and still being smoked today.

This New World genus includes N. tabacum, *the plant used for cigarette tobacco.*

Planting

Seeding: Indoors in early spring; direct sow later

Planting out: Once soil has warmed

Spacing: 8–12"

Growing

Flowering tobaccos will grow equally well in **full sun** and **light or partial shade**. The soil should be **fertile,** high in **organic matter, moist** and **well drained**. The seeds require light for germination, so leave them uncovered.

Tips

These plants are popular in beds and borders. The dwarf varieties do well in containers.

Do not plant flowering tobaccos near tomatoes because they are members of the same plant family and share many of the same diseases. The *Nicotiana* may attract and harbor diseases that can kill tomatoes but will hardly affect the flowering tobacco.

Like sweet peas, the flowering tobaccos were first cultivated for their wonderfully scented flowers. The flowers were then available only in a greenish color, and they opened only in the evening and at night. In attempts to expand the variety of colors and have the flowers open during the day, the popular scent has, in some cases, been lost.

Nicki Series (above) & with *N. sylvestris* (below)

N. x sanderae (above), *N. sylvestris* (below)

Recommended

N. **Hummingbird Series** includes compact plants growing 6–12" tall and 10" wide. The fragrant flowers come in red, pink, lilac, green and white. This series is excellent at the front of a border or massed.

N. langsdorffii grows up to 3–5' tall. It bears clusters of bell-shaped, green, unscented flowers. The leaves and stems are hairy and feel sticky to the touch.

N. x *sanderae (N. alata* x *N. forgetiana)* is a hybrid that grows 2–5' tall and 12–16" wide. The parents are fragrant, but the hybrid and its cultivars are lightly scented to scentless. **'Avalon Bright Pink'** is a well-branched plant that grows 8–12" tall. It bears an abundance of vibrant pink flowers that contrast nicely with its dark green foliage. **Domino Series** plants are compact and grow 12–18" tall, with an equal spread. Flowers come in many colors and stay open all day. **Merlin Series** has dwarf plants ideal for mixed planters. The flowers may be red, pink, purple, white or pale green. **Nicki Series** has fragrant blooms in many colors, and the flowers stay open all day. The compact plants grow up to 18" tall. **'Only the Lonely'** grows up to 4' tall and bears white blooms that are scented in the evening. Plants in the **Sensation Series** grow up to 30" tall and bear red, white or pink flowers that stay open all day.

N. sylvestris grows up to 4' tall and 24" wide. Its white blooms give off a scent in the evening.

Problems & Pests

Tobacco mosiac virus, aphids, whiteflies and downy or powdery mildew may cause occasional problems.

Ingesting the leaves of any Nicotiana *species can cause severe poisoning and even death.*

N. sylvestris

Four-O'Clock Flower

Marvel of Peru
Mirabilis

Height: 18–36" **Spread:** 18–24" **Flower color:** red, pink, magenta, yellow, white or bicolored

IF YOUR COLOR-RIOT QUOTIENT NEEDS A BOOST, HERE'S A PLANT that will help. Many colorful hues can appear on the same plant. With a rather robust (some would say unruly) habit, four-o'clock flower brings a fullness to any flower bed. The fragrance is a plus. But why does this plant show up for work so late? The blooms, which usually open in the late afternoon, attract nocturnal insects for pollination and remain open all night or until they have had an appropriate visitor.

Planting

Seeding: Indoors in late winter; direct sow in mid-spring

Planting out: Mid-spring

Spacing: 16–24"

Growing

Four-o'clock flower prefers **full sun** but tolerates partial shade. The soil should ideally be **fertile,** though any **well-drained** soil is tolerated.

This plant is a perennial that is treated as an annual, and it may be grown from tuberous roots. Dig up the tuberous roots in fall and replant in spring. Some tubers may survive winters in southern parts of Illinois. Four-o'clock flower also freely self-seeds and may become weedy if allowed to renew itself in spring.

Tips

Use four-o'clock flower in beds, borders, containers and window boxes. The flowers are scented, so the plant is often located near patios or terraces where the scent can be enjoyed in the afternoon and evening.

Recommended

M. jalapa forms a bushy mound of foliage. The flowers may be solid or bicolored. A single plant may bear flowers of several colors.

Problems & Pests

This plant has very few problems as long as it is given well-drained soil.

This tropical plant is native to Central and South America. Its roots and seeds are poisonous.

Many species of moths are attracted to the blooms of four-o'clock flower, which may appear in several colors on a single plant.

Fuchsia

Fuchsia

Height: 6–36" **Spread:** 6–36" **Flower color:** pink, orange, red, purple or white; often bicolored

'IT'S *FOOK-SEE-A*,' MY FRIEND WOULD ALWAYS BELLOW WHENEVER he heard the more common pronunciation. Whoever is right, I preferred his pronunciation because it sounded more like a plant and less like a designer color. Most often seen as multi-colored double blooms in spectacular hanging baskets, fuchsia varieties come with single flowers and variegated foliage as well. Try one as a challenge to your gardening acumen—or as one of your chief 'nags' to remind you to water.

Some gardeners who have kept fuchsias over several years have trained the plants to adopt a tree form.

Planting

Seeding: Not recommended

Planting out: After last frost

Spacing: 12–24"

Growing

Fuchsias are grown in **partial or light shade**. They are generally not tolerant of summer heat, and full sun can be too hot for them. The soil should be **fertile, moist** and **well drained**.

Fuchsias need to be well watered, particularly in hot weather. Ensure that the soil has good drainage because otherwise the plants can develop rot problems. Fuchsias planted in well-aerated soil with lots of perlite are almost impossible to overwater. These plants bloom on new growth, which will be stimulated by a high-nitrogen plant food.

Although fuchsias are hard to start from seed, they are easy to propagate from cuttings. Snip off 6" of new tip growth, remove the leaves from the lower third of the stem and insert the cuttings into soft soil or perlite. Once rooted and potted, the plants will bloom all summer.

Tips

Upright fuchsias can be used in mixed planters, beds and borders. Pendulous fuchsias are most often used in hanging baskets, but these plants, with their flowers dangling from flexible branches, also make attractive additions to planters and rock gardens.

'Winston Churchill' (above)

Fuchsias should be deadheaded. Pluck the swollen seedpods from behind the fading petals or the seeds will ripen, thereby robbing the plant of energy necessary for flower production.

Fuchsias are perennials that are grown as annuals. To store fuchsias over winter, cut back the plants to 6" stumps after the first light frost and place them in a dark, cold, but not freezing location. Water just enough to keep the soil barely moist, and do not feed. In mid-spring, repot the stumps, set them near a bright window and fertilize them lightly. Set your overwintered plants outdoors the following spring after all danger of frost has passed.

Recommended

F. **Angels' Earrings Series** from Proven Winners includes very heat- and humidity-tolerant plants that grow 10–12" tall. **'Cascading Angel's Earrings'** has large, abundant flowers with red sepals and purple-blue petals. **'Dainty Angel's Earrings'** is a more upright plant than others in the series. The flowers have shiny red sepals and purple-blue petals. **'Snow Fire'** has a semi-trailing habit and bears bright red and white flowers.

F. x *hybrida* includes dozens of cultivars; just a few examples are given here. The upright fuchsias grow 18–36" tall, and the pendulous fuchsias grow 6–24" tall. Many available hybrids cannot be started from seed. **'Deep Purple'** has purple petals and white sepals. **'Gartenmeister Bonstedt'** is an upright, shrubby cultivar that grows about 24" tall and bears tubular, orange-red flowers. The foliage is bronzy red with purple undersides. **'Snowburner'** has white petals and pink sepals. **'Swingtime'** has white petals with pink bases and pink sepals. This plant grows 12–24" tall and spreads about 6". It can be grown in a hanging basket or as a relaxed upright plant in beds and borders. **'Winston Churchill'** has purple petals and pink sepals. The plant grows 8–30" tall, with an equal spread. It is quite upright in form but is often grown in hanging baskets.

Problems & Pests

Aphids, spider mites and whiteflies are common insect pests. Diseases such as crown rot, root rot and rust can be avoided with good air circulation and drainage.

Children, and some adults, enjoy popping the fat buds of fuchsias. The temptation to squeeze them is almost irresistible.

'Snowburner'

Gazania

Gazania

Height: usually 6–8"; may reach 12–18" **Spread:** 8–12"
Flower color: red, orange, yellow, pink, cream

DARK, CONTRASTING RINGS NEAR THE CENTER OF THE PETALS OF large, nearly flat flowers make gazania stand out in almost any type of planting. Containers sparkle when these flowers are grown well. Another super attribute is the ability of gazania to deal with a fair amount of drought.

This native of southern Africa has very few pests and transplants easily, even when blooming.

Planting

Seeding: Indoors in late winter; direct sow after last frost

Planting out: After last frost

Spacing: 6–10"

Growing

Gazania grows best in **full sun** but tolerates some shade. The soil should be of **poor to average fertility, sandy** and **well drained**. This plant grows best in hot weather over 80° F.

Tips

Low-growing gazania makes an excellent groundcover and is also useful on exposed slopes, in mixed containers and as an edging in flowerbeds.

Daybreak Series (above), other cultivars (below)

Recommended

G. rigens forms a low basal rosette of lobed foliage. Large, daisy-like flowers with pointed petals are borne on strong stems above the plant. The petals often have a contrasting stripe or spot. The flowers tend to close on gloomy days and in low-light situations. The species is rarely grown, but several hybrid cultivars are available. Plants of the **Daybreak Series** bear flowers in many colors, often with a contrasting stripe down the center of each petal. These flowers will stay open on dull days but close on rainy or very dark days. **Kiss Series** has compact plants with large flowers in several colors. Seeds are available by individual flower color or as a mix. **Mini-Star Series** also has compact plants. The flowers are in many colors with a contrasting dot at the base of each petal. **'Sundance'** bears flowers in reds and yellows with dark, contrasting stripes down the centers of the petals.

Problems & Pests

Overwatering is the likely cause of any problems for this plant.

Geranium

Pelargonium

Height: 8–36" **Spread:** 6"–4' **Flower color:** red, pink, violet, orange, salmon, white, purple

THE STOCK-IN-TRADE OF THE BEDDING PLANT INDUSTRY, geraniums suffer only from garden snobs who find them too common. But go to a plant trial facility and see how many varieties are being developed. You will discover that it is always possible to improve on a good plant. Look for deep zoning (banding) in the foliage or for an unusual flower attribute— some have 'freckles' on their petals. The ivy-leaved types are great in hanging baskets. And then there are the scented geraniums—a world unto themselves. Choices? Many.

The name Pelargonium arises from the Greek word pelargos, 'stork,' referring to the similarity between a stork's bill and the shape of the fruit.

Planting

Seeding: Indoors in early winter

Planting out: After last frost

Spacing: Zonal geranium, about 12";
ivy-leaved geranium, 24–36";
scented geraniums, 12–36"

Growing

Geraniums prefer **full sun** but tolerate partial shade, although they may not bloom as profusely. The soil should be **fertile** and **well drained**.

Geraniums are slow to grow from seed, so purchasing plants may prove easier. However, if you would like to try starting your own from seed, start them indoors in early winter and cover them with clear plastic to maintain humidity until they germinate. Once the seedlings have three or four leaves, transplant them into individual 3–4" pots. Keep them in bright locations because they need lots of light to maintain their compact shape.

Deadheading is essential to keep geraniums blooming and looking neat. The flowerheads are attached to long stems that break off easily where they attach to the plant. Some gardeners prefer to snip off just the flowering end in order to avoid potentially damaging the plant.

Tips

Geraniums are very popular bedding plants. Use zonal geranium in beds, borders and containers. Ivy-leaved geranium is most often used in hanging baskets and containers to take advantage of its trailing habit, but it is also interesting used as a bedding plant to form a bushy,

'Peppermint' (above)

Scented cultivar (center), *P. peltatum* (below)

P. zonale cultivar

P. zonale (zonal geranium) grows up to 24" tall and 12" wide. Dwarf varieties grow up to 8" tall and 6" wide. The flowers are red, pink, purple, orange or white. **Fireworks Series** is a unique new class of geranium hybrids with maple-shaped leaves and flowers that look like fireworks exploding. They are heat tolerant and great in containers. **Orbit Series** has attractive, early-blooming, compact plants. The seed is often sold in a mixed packet, but some individual colors are available. **Pillar Series** includes upright plants that grow up to 36" tall with staking. Salmon, violet and orange flowers are available. **Pinto Series** is available in all colors, and seed is generally sold by the color so you don't have to buy a mix and hope you like what you get.

P. **species and cultivars** (scented geraniums, scented pelargoniums) comprise a large number of geraniums that have scented leaves. The scent categories are rose, mint, citrus, fruit, spice and pungent. In the following list, a parent of each cultivar is indicated in parentheses. Some cultivars, such as 'Apple' (*P. odoratissimum*), readily self-seed and stay true to form, but most must be propagated by cuttings to retain their ornamental and fragrant qualities. Many cultivars have variegated leaves. Intensely scented cultivars include 'Chocolate-Mint' (*P. quercifolium*), 'Lemon' (*P. crispum*), 'Lime' (*P.* x *nervosum*), 'Old-Fashioned Rose' (*P. graveolens*), 'Peppermint' (*P. tomentosum*), 'Pine' (*P. denticulatum*), 'Prince Rupert' (*P. crispum*) and 'Rober's Lemon Rose' (*P. graveolens*).

spreading groundcover. Scented geraniums are great for containers, especially on a deck or patio where they can be placed so you can enjoy their wonderful aromas.

Geraniums are perennials that are treated as annuals. They can be kept indoors over winter in a bright room.

Recommended

The following species and varieties are some of the easier ones to start from seed. Many popular varieties can be propagated only from cuttings and must be purchased as plants.

P. peltatum (ivy-leaved geranium) grows up to 12" tall and up to 4' wide. Many colors are available. Plants in the **Summer Showers Series** can take four or more months to flower from seed. The **Tornado Series** is very good for hanging baskets and containers. The plants are quite compact, with flowers in either lilac or white.

Problems & Pests

Aphids will flock to overfertilized plants, but the insects can usually be washed off before they do much damage. Leaf spot and blight may bother geraniums growing in cool, moist soil.

Edema is an unusual condition to which geraniums are susceptible. This disease occurs when a plant is overwatered and the leaf cells burst. A warty surface then develops on the leaves. There is no cure, but the problem can be avoided by watering carefully and removing any damaged leaves as the plant grows. The condition is more common in ivy-leaved geranium.

Ivy-leaved geranium is one of the most beautiful plants to include in a mixed hanging basket.

P. zonale cultivar (above), *P. peltatum* (below)

Globe Amaranth

Gomphrena

Height: 6–30" **Spread:** 6–15" **Flower color:** purple, orange, magenta, pink, white, sometimes red

'EVERLASTING' IS A TERM OFTEN USED SYNONYMOUSLY WITH globe amaranth. The neat, tight-knit blooms atop sturdy stalks are prime candidates for drying and use in arrangements. Use this plant in the sunniest, hottest spot in the garden because it relishes the heat.

Planting

Seeding: Indoors in late winter

Planting out: After last frost

Spacing: 10"

Globe amaranth flowers are popular for cutting and drying because they keep their color and form well when dried. Pick the flowers before they are completely open and dry them upside down in a cool, dry location.

Growing

Globe amaranth prefers **full sun**. The soil should be of **average fertility** and **well drained**. This plant likes hot weather. It needs watering only when drought conditions persist.

Seeds will germinate more quickly if soaked in water for two to four days before sowing. They need warm soil above 70° F to sprout.

The long-lasting flowers require only occasional deadheading.

Tips

Use globe amaranth in an informal or cottage garden. This plant is often underused because it doesn't start flowering until later in summer than many other annuals. Don't overlook it—the blooms are worth the wait and provide color from the middle of summer until the first frost.

Recommended

G. globosa forms a rounded, bushy plant, 12–24" tall, that is dotted with papery, clover-like blossoms in purple, magenta, white or pink. '**Buddy**' has more compact plants, 6–12" tall, with deep purple flowers. '**Gnome Mixed**' grows 6–12" tall and has flowers in shades of white, pink and rosy purple. '**Lavender Lady**' becomes a large plant, up to 24" tall, and bears lavender purple flowers.

G. '**Strawberry Fields**' is a hybrid with bright orange-red or red flowers. It grows about 30" tall and spreads about half as much.

Problems & Pests

Watch for some fungal diseases, such as gray mold and leaf spot.

G. globosa (above & with *Tropaeolum,* below)

The clover-like heads actually consist of showy bracts (modified leaves) from which the tiny flowers emerge.

Heliotrope
Cherry Pie Plant
Heliotropium

Height: 8"–4' **Spread:** 12–24" **Flower color:** purple, blue, white

HELIOTROPE PROVIDES LOVELY DEEP BLUE TO PURPLE FLOWERS that can saturate the garden with their color and fragrance. The alternative common name refers to the floral scent, although vanilla is perhaps the more often used comparison. White varieties of heliotrope are also available, with some easily as fragrant as their bluish cousins, if not more so. Older varieties are often more scented, while newer varieties are bred for garden performance.

Planting

Seeding: Indoors in mid-winter

Planting out: Once soil has warmed

Spacing: 12–18"

Growing

Heliotrope grows best in **full sun.** The soil should be **fertile,** rich in **organic matter, moist** and **well drained.** Although overwatering will kill heliotrope, the plant will also be slow to recover if left to dry to the point of wilting.

Heliotrope is sensitive to cold weather, so plant it out after all danger of frost has passed. Protect plants with newspaper or a floating row cover (available at garden centers) if an unexpected late frost or cold snap should arrive. Container-grown plants can be brought indoors at night if frost is expected.

H. arborescens (all photos)

This old-fashioned flower may have been popular in your grandmother's day. Its recent return to popularity comes as no surprise considering its attractive foliage, flowers and scent.

Tips

Heliotrope is ideal for growing in containers or beds near windows and patios where the wonderful scent of the flowers can be enjoyed. 'Atlantis' and 'Nagano' are very heat-tolerant selections that do particularly well in containers and hanging baskets.

This plant can be shaped into a tree form, or standard, by pinching off the lower branches as the plant grows until it reaches the desired height and then pinching the top to encourage the plant to bush out. Create a shorter, bushy form by pinching all the tips that develop.

Heliotrope can be grown indoors as a houseplant in a sunny window. A plant may survive for years if kept outdoors all summer and indoors all winter in a cool, bright room.

Recommended

H. arborescens is a low, bushy shrub that is treated as an annual. It grows 18–24" tall, with an equal spread. Large clusters of purple, blue or white, scented flowers are produced all summer. Some new cultivars are not as strongly scented as the species. 'Atlantis' is a heat-tolerant plant from Proven Winners that grows 10–12" tall and bears violet blue flowers. 'Blue Wonder' is a compact plant that was developed for heavily scented flowers. Plants grow up to 16" tall with dark purple flowers. 'Dwarf Marine' ('Mini Marine') is a compact, bushy plant with fragrant, purple flowers. It grows 8–12" tall and also makes a good houseplant for a bright location. 'Fragrant Delight' is an older cultivar with royal purple flowers of intense fragrance. It grows 24–36" tall and may reach a height of 4' if grown as a standard. 'Marine' has violet blue flowers and grows about 18" tall. 'Nagano,' from Proven Winners, grows vigorously to 12–14" tall, producing deep purple flowers. 'White Delight' is similar to 'Fragrant Delight,' but with white flowers and a stronger scent. It grows 18–24" tall.

Plants that are a little underwatered tend to have a stronger scent.

Problems & Pests

Aphids and whiteflies can be problems for heliotrope.

Heliotrope is rarely troubled by diseases, requires little maintenance and attracts butterflies with its lovely scented blooms. Try it in a patio pot or hanging basket with other sun-lovers, such as bidens or petunia.

Hollyhock

Alcea

Height: 5–8' **Spread:** 24" **Flower color:** yellow, cream, white, apricot, rose, pink, red, purple, reddish black

IF YOU'RE OF A CERTAIN AGE, YOU GREW UP WITH THREE stalks of hollyhock in a row across the back of your house, looking raggedy at best and awful most of the time. Newer cultivars deal with the most obvious flaws, but you can still commit that gardening faux pas common in days gone by. A better thought: use hollyhocks as the vertical accent in a mixed border.

Planting

Seeding: Start indoors in mid-winter

Planting out: After last frost

Spacing: 18–24"

Growing

Hollyhocks prefer **full sun** but tolerate partial shade. The soil should be **average to rich** and **well drained**. Plant hollyhocks in a different part of the garden each year to keep hollyhock rust at bay.

A. rosea *was originally grown as a food plant. The young leaves were added to salads.*

Tips

Because they are so tall, hollyhocks look best at the back of the border or in the center of an island bed. In a windy location they will need to be staked. Plant them against a fence or wall for support. If the main stem is pinched out early in the season, hollyhocks will be shorter and bushier with smaller flower spikes. These shorter stems are less likely to be broken by wind and can be left unstaked.

Old-fashioned types typically have single flowers, and they grow much taller than newer varieties. Self-sown seedlings are often very tough and durable plants.

Recommended

A. rosea forms a rosette of basal leaves. The tall flowering stalk bears ruffled single or double blooms. '**Nigra**' bears reddish black single flowers with yellow centers. '**Single Mixed**' bears carmine, pink, rose, cream or white flowers that look like hibiscus blossoms.

A. rugosa (Russian hollyhock) is similar to *A. rosea* but is more resistant to hollyhock rust. It bears pale yellow to orangy yellow single flowers.

Problems & Pests

Hollyhock rust is the biggest problem. Hollyhocks are also susceptible to bacterial and fungal leaf spot. Slugs and cutworms occasionally attack young growth. Sometimes mallow flea beetles, aphids and Japanese beetles cause trouble.

A. rosea 'Single Mixed'

The roots of a hollyhock relative, the marsh mallow (A. officinalis), were once used to make laxatives and throat lozenges. Now popular campfire treats, 'marshmallows' no longer contain mallow or have its medicinal properties.

A. rosea 'Nigra'

Hyacinth Bean

Egyptian Bean, Lablab Bean

Lablab (Dolichos)

Height: 10–15' **Spread:** variable **Flower color:** purple, white; plant also grown for purple pods

THINK OF HYACINTH BEAN AS A sweet pea on steroids. The vines grow profusely, supporting the reddish purple flowers and, later, the iridescent purple pods that give the plant its characteristic look.

Grow sweet peas if you want fragrance; grow hyacinth bean if you want great visual interest and seedpods that, when cooked carefully, can double as a food crop.

Planting

Seeding: Direct sow around last-frost date, or start indoors in peat pots in early spring

Planting out: After last frost

Spacing: 12–18"

Growing

Hyacinth bean prefers **full sun.** The soil should be **average to fertile, moist** and **well drained.** Feed this plant weekly to encourage plentiful flowering.

Tips

Hyacinth bean needs a trellis, net, pole or other supporting structure to twine up. Plant it against a fence or near a balcony.

The raw beans contain a cyanide-releasing chemical. Boiling and changing the water several times removes the toxin.

Recommended

L. purpureus (Dolichos lablab) is a vigorous twining vine. It can grow up to 30' tall, but when grown as an annual it reaches about 10–15'. It bears many purple or white flowers over the summer, followed by deep purple pods.

Problems & Pests

Rare problems with leaf spot can occur.

Thomas Jefferson is said to have built a special arbor so that he could grow and enjoy hyacinth bean in the garden at Monticello.

The purple pods are edible if thoroughly cooked with two to four changes of water. Try adding them to a stir-fry for some unusual color.

Impatiens

Impatiens

Height: 6–36" **Spread:** 8–24" **Flower color:** shades of purple, red, burgundy, pink, yellow, orange, apricot, white; also bicolored and picotee

EASILY ONE OF THE MOST ASKED QUESTIONS IN GARDENING IS how to get more color in the shade without having to use impatiens. The answer may be close at hand: try one of the impatiens you haven't considered before. Touring a seed company's greenhouse one day, I ventured an opinion that double-flowering impatiens were very beautiful and might one day rival the single-flowered types. They were novelty types, I was told. Over the years it has been affirming to see how much breeding work has helped these varieties, and how sales of them have skyrocketed. The flowers look like miniature roses.

Planting

Seeding: Indoors in mid-winter; balsam impatiens indoors in late winter

Planting out: Once soil has warmed

Spacing: 12–18"

Growing

Impatiens do best in **partial shade** but most tolerate full shade. If kept moist, some will tolerate full sun. Balsam impatiens is the best adapted to sunny locations. New Guinea impatiens does well with morning sun but will require afternoon shade. The soil should be **fertile, humus rich, moist** and **well drained**. New Guinea impatiens does not like wet feet, so good drainage is a must.

Don't cover the seeds—they germinate best when exposed to light.

Tips

Busy Lizzie is known for its ability to grow and flower profusely in even deep shade. Mass plant in beds under trees, along shady fences or walls, or in porch planters. It also looks lovely in hanging baskets. The new double-flowering varieties, such as those in the Fiesta Series, work beautifully as accent plants in hosta and wildflower gardens.

New Guinea impatiens is almost shrubby in form and is popular in patio planters, beds and borders. This plant is grown as much for its variegated leaves as for its flowers.

Balsam impatiens was a popular garden plant in the Victorian era and has recently experienced a resurgence in popularity. The habit of this plant is more upright than that of

I. balsamina (above),
I. walleriana with *Coleus* & *Ipomoea batatas* (below)

I. hawkeri New Guinea Hybrids (photos this page)

most other impatiens, and it is attractive when grouped in beds and borders.

Recommended

New impatiens varieties are introduced every year, expanding the selection of size, form and color. The following list includes varieties that are popular year after year.

I. balsamina (balsam impatiens) grows 12–36" tall and up to 18" wide. The flowers come in shades of purple, red, pink or white. There are several double-flowered cultivars, such as 'Camellia-flowered,' with pink, red or white flowers on plants up to 24" tall; 'Tom Thumb,' with pink, red, purple or white flowers on compact plants to 12" tall; and 'Topknot,' with large flowers in a similar range of colors held above the foliage on plants 12" tall.

I. hawkeri New Guinea Hybrids (New Guinea impatiens) grow 12–30" tall and 12" wide or wider. The flowers come in shades of red, orange, pink, purple or white. The foliage is often variegated with a yellow stripe down the center of each leaf. Celebration Series includes plants 15–30" tall with flowers in many reddish shades.

I. Seashell Series is a group of new African hybrids with flowers in shades of yellow, orange, apricot and pink. Plants grow 8–10" tall and spread about 12".

I. walleriana (busy Lizzie) grows 6–18" tall and up to 24" wide. The flowers come in shades of red, orange, pink, purple or white, or are bicolored. Dazzler Series are compact varieties growing 10–14" tall and 8–10" wide. They stay covered in blooms of numerous colors. **Fiesta Series** includes compact plants about 12" tall, with an equal spread. They bear double flowers in shades of pink, orange, red and burgundy. With their habit and flower form, they resemble small rose bushes. **Mosaic Series** plants have uniquely colored flowers, with the margins and most of the petals speckled in a darker shade of the petal color. **Super Elfin Series** is a common group of cultivars. The flowers come in many shades, including bicolors. The compact plants grow about 12" tall, but they may spread more. **Swirl Series** plants have unusual picotee patterns on the flower petals. **'Victorian Rose'** is an All-America Selections winner with deep pink double or semi-double flowers.

Problems & Pests

Fungal leaf spot, stem rot, thrips, *Verticillium* wilt, whiteflies and aphids can cause trouble.

I. walleriana (photos this page)

With their reliable blooming in shade, and their wide variety of colors and types, impatiens are America's top-selling bedding plants.

Lantana
Shrub Verbena
Lantana

Height: 6–42" **Spread:** 12–42" **Flower color:** yellow, orange, pink, purple, red, white; often in combination

LANTANAS GAIN POPULARITY EVERY YEAR BECAUSE OF THEIR range and combinations of flower colors as well as their low-maintenance requirements. The flowers often start as one color in the bud stage and mature to a different color, creating a striking display as several colors may appear in a cluster at once. The informal, sprawling habit of lantanas adds to their charm, as does their ability to attract butterflies.

Planting

Seeding: Not recommended

Planting out: Into warm soil after danger of frost has passed

Spacing: 2–4'

Growing

Lantanas grow best in **full sun** but tolerate partial shade. They prefer soil that is **fertile, moist** and **well drained** but can handle heat and drought. Take cuttings in late summer if you would like plants for the following summer but don't want to store a large one over winter.

Tips

Lantanas are tender shrubs grown as annuals. They are useful in beds, borders, mixed containers and hanging baskets. These plants can handle heat, making them perfect for low-maintenance gardens.

Recommended

L. camara is a bushy plant that bears round clusters of flowers in many colors. It is rarely grown in favor of the cultivars. Plants in the **Lucky Series** grow 10–14" tall and have a neat upright habit. In the series are 'Lemon Cream,' 'Peach Sunrise,' 'Pot of Gold' and 'Red Hot.' Lucky Series plants do well in the heat and with restricted water. **'New Gold'** grows 24" tall and bears clusters of bright yellow flowers.

L. montevidensis (weeping lantana) is a weak-stemmed, trailing shrub. **'Samantha'** is a semi-trailing plant growing 6–12" tall and spreading to 24" wide. It has creamy yellow flowers and yellow-margined green leaves. **'Weeping Lavender'** grows 6–12" tall with slender stems that trail to 36" long. It bears dense clusters of pinkish lilac flowers.

L. **Patriot Series** includes plants that flower in a wide range of colors. The

L. camara cultivar

Lantanas are not intimidated by hot, dry weather, and a 3" bedding plant can reach the size of a small shrub in a single season.

dark to mid-green foliage has a minty fragrance. **'Dove Wings'** gracefully grows 24" tall and 12" wide, producing pure white flowers. **'Hallelujah'** grows 42" tall and wide. Flowers change from yellow-gold to orange-pink and finally lavender. **'Hot Country'** grows 36" tall and wide and produces sienna yellow blooms that mature quickly to fuchsia. **'Rainbow'** is a compact plant growing 12" tall and wide. It has large, dark green leaves and yellow, orange and pink flowers.

Problems & Pests

Lantana is subject to infestations of whiteflies.

Larkspur

Rocket Larkspur, Annual Delphinium

Consolida

Height: 1–4' **Spread:** 6–14" **Flower color:** blue, purple, pink, white

WHETHER YOU'RE SEEKING A COTTAGE-GARDEN LOOK OR MORE vertical lines in your mixed border, larkspur fits the bill with its fern-like foliage and small flowers displayed along upright stems. Often lumped botanically with *Delphinium,* the annual larkspur can resemble its perennial cousins. It also shares some of the delphiniums' distaste for heat, putting forth its best flowers in cooler conditions.

Planting

Seeding: Indoors in mid-winter; direct sow in early or mid-spring, as soon as soil can be worked

Planting out: Mid-spring

Spacing: 12"

Growing

Larkspur does equally well in **full sun** or **light shade**. The soil should be **fertile,** rich in **organic matter** and **well drained.** Keep the roots cool and add a light mulch; dried grass clippings or shredded leaves work well. Don't put mulch too close to the base of the plant or the plant may develop crown rot.

Plant seeds in peat pots to prevent root damage when the seedlings are transplanted. Seeds started indoors may benefit from being chilled in the refrigerator for one week prior to sowing.

Deadhead to keep larkspur blooming well into fall.

Tips

Plant groups of larkspur in mixed borders or cottage gardens. The tallest varieties may require staking to stay upright.

Recommended

C. ambigua (*C. ajacis*) is an upright plant with feathery foliage. It bears spikes of purple, blue, pink or white flowers. **Dwarf Rocket Series** includes plants that grow 12–20" tall and 6–10" wide and bloom in many colors. '**Earl Grey**' grows 3–4' tall and bears flowers in an intriguing color between slate gray and gunmetal gray. '**Frosted Skies**' grows to

C. ambigua

18" tall and bears large, semi-double flowers in a beautiful bicolor of blue and white. **Giant Imperial Series** flower in many colors, on plants 24–36" tall and up to 14" wide. **Sydney Series** plants grow 4' tall and 10–14" wide. They bear spikes of long-lasting double flowers $1^{1}/_{2}$" across, in purple, rose or white.

Problems & Pests

Slugs and snails are potential troublemakers. Powdery mildew and crown or root rot are avoidable if you water thoroughly, but not too often, and make sure the plants have good air circulation.

Lavatera
Annual Mallow
Lavatera

Height: 18"–4' **Spread:** 18–24" **Flower color:** pink, salmon, white, red, purple

DAPPLED, SAUCER-SHAPED FLOWERS TOP THIS HANDSOME PLANT, most often in shades of pink. With its Mediterranean heritage, lavatera is adapted to hot, dry summers, but it can die out in our hottest, humid weather. Still, its multiple flowers and attractive foliage more than make up for whatever it lacks in long-season performance. Watch how the furled petals unfold, a characteristic lavatera shares with okra and other plants in the mallow family.

Lavatera is often called annual mallow, and it is in the same family as the true mallows (genus Malva).

Planting

Seeding: Direct sow in spring, or start indoors in late winter

Planting out: After last frost

Spacing: 18–24"

Growing

Lavatera prefers **full sun** but needs some shade in warmer areas of the state. The soil should be of **average fertility, light** and **well drained**.

This plant resents having its roots disturbed and tends to do better when direct sown. If you start seeds indoors, use peat pots.

Tips

Lavatera can be used as a colorful backdrop behind smaller plants in a bed or border. The blooms make attractive cut flowers and are edible. Lavatera grows to be fairly large and shrubby, so stake tall varieties to keep them from falling over in summer rain showers.

Recommended

L. trimestris is a bushy plant up to 4' tall and 18–24" wide. It bears red, pink or white, funnel-shaped flowers. **Beauty Series** includes 'Pink Beauty,' growing 24" tall with light pink flowers; 'Rose Beauty,' growing 24–30" tall with rose pink flowers; 'Salmon Beauty,' growing 24–30" tall with salmon pink flowers; and 'White Beauty,' growing 18–24" tall with white flowers. **'Mont Blanc'** bears white flowers on compact plants that grow to about 20" tall. 'Silver Cup' grows 24–30" tall and has large, cup-shaped, light pink flowers with dark pink veins.

'Silver Cup' (above), 'Mont Blanc' (below)

Problems & Pests

Plant lavatera in well-drained soil to avoid root rot. Destroy any rust-infected plants. This plant may attract Japanese beetles.

Licorice Plant
False Licorice
Helichrysum

Height: 6–24" **Spread:** 18–36" **Flower color:** yellow-white; plant grown for foliage

IF YOU EVER SPOT AN OVER-THE-TOP CONTAINER PLANTING, chances are there's licorice plant in it somewhere. For plants that don't typically flower, licorice plants bring great contrast to any combination planting because of their distinctive silver shades and rounded leaves on long stems.

Planting
Seeding: Not recommended

Planting out: After last frost

Spacing: About 30"

Growing
Licorice plants prefer **full sun**. The soil should be of **poor to average fertility, neutral or alkaline** and **well drained**. Licorice plants wilt when the soil dries but revive quickly once watered. They are rampant growers, but a few snips with a hand pruner will quickly bring them in line.

Take cuttings in fall for new plants the following spring. Once they have rooted, keep the young plants in a cool, bright room for winter.

Tips

Licorice plants are perennials grown as annuals. They are prized for their foliage rather than flowers. Include them in your hanging baskets and containers, and the trailing growth will quickly fill in and provide a soft, silvery backdrop for the colorful flowers of other plants. Licorice plants can also be used as annual groundcovers or as edging plants. They will cascade down in a silvery wave over rocks and retaining walls.

These plants are good watering indicators for hanging baskets. When you see your licorice plant wilting, get out the hose or watering can.

'White Licorice' (above)

'Silver' with *Verbena* & *Ricinus communis*

Recommended

H. petiolare is a trailing plant up to 36" in spread, with fuzzy gray-green leaves. Cultivars are more common than the species. The following four cultivars grow 6–9" tall and 18–24" wide: **'Licorice Splash'** is a bushy plant with pale green and white variegated foliage; **'Limelight'** has bright chartreuse leaves that need protection from direct sun to maintain their color; **'Petite Licorice'** is very compact with dusty white leaves; **'White Licorice'** is a vigorous plant with silver-frosted green leaves. **'Petiolatum'** grows 18–24" tall and has silvery green foliage. **'Silver'** is a common cultivar with gray-green leaves covered in silvery down. **'Variegatum'** grows 18–24" tall and has gray-green leaves dappled or margined in silvery cream.

H. thianschanicum **'Icicles'** is a compact plant 10–15" tall, with narrow, velvety, silver leaves and rare yellow to orange flowers. Its mounding habit makes it great for mixed containers. It is occasionally winter hardy in well-drained areas.

Problems & Pests

Leaf-feeding caterpillars can be a problem. Powdery mildew occurs occasionally, though you might not see it because the leaves are already soft and white.

Lobelia
Edging Lobelia
Lobelia

Height: 3–10" **Spread:** equal to or twice the height **Flower color:** purple, blue, pink, white, red

THE MANY TRAILING VARIETIES OF THIS COMMON BEDDING PLANT have helped increase its popularity, although there are many upright versions as well. Its compact nature and heavy flowering make it a good choice for edging, but you will find it most often in hanging baskets in garden centers in spring.

Planting

Seeding: Indoors in mid-winter

Planting out: After last frost

Spacing: 6"

Growing

Lobelia grows well in **full sun** or **partial shade**. The soil should be **fertile**, high in **organic matter, moist** and fairly **well drained**. Lobelia likes cool summer nights. In hot weather, take care that its soil stays moist.

Lobelia seedlings are susceptible to damping-off. See the 'Annuals from Seed' section in the introduction to this book for information on proper propagation techniques to help avoid damping-off.

Cascade Series (above), 'Sapphire' (below)

Tips

Use lobelia along the edges of beds and borders, on rock walls, in rock gardens, in mixed containers or in hanging baskets.

Trim lobelia back after the first wave of flowers. It will stop blooming in the hottest part of summer but usually revives in fall.

Recommended

L. erinus may be rounded and bushy or low and trailing. It bears blue to violet flowers with yellow to white throats. **'Big Blue'** flowers well through the season. **Cascade Series** is a trailing form with flowers in many shades. **'Crystal Palace'** is a compact plant that rarely grows over 4" in height. This cultivar has dark green foliage and dark blue flowers. **'Laguna Compact Blue with Eye'** is the most heat-tolerant variety to date. It grows to 10" tall and produces sky blue flowers. **'Laguna Pink'** has dusky pink flowers that trail out of pots and baskets. It grows to 6" tall and 14" wide and is very heat tolerant. **Regatta Series** is a trailing cultivar that tolerates heat well and blooms longer than many other cultivars. **Riviera Series** is only 3–4" tall and has flowers in blue and purple on bushy plants. **'Sapphire'** has white-centered blue flowers on trailing plants.

Problems & Pests

Rust, leaf spot and slugs may be troublesome.

Love-in-a-Mist

Nigella

Height: 16–24" **Spread:** 8–12" **Flower color:** blue, white, pink, purple

ONE TEST FOR AN ANNUAL IS WHETHER THE PLANT CAN SERVE more than one purpose. Love-in-a-mist passes this test with flying colors: it serves as a fine foil in a bedding situation for plants with bolder foliage, such as dusty miller; its flowers can be used in fresh bouquets; and its seedpods are often harvested for dried arrangements. If you're into the cottage look, love-in-a-mist is a great choice.

Planting

Seeding: Indoors in late winter; direct sow in early spring

Planting out: Mid-spring

Spacing: 10–15"

Love-in-a-mist has a tendency to self-sow and may show up in unexpected spots in your garden for years to come.

Growing

Love-in-a-mist prefers **full sun**. The soil should be of **average fertility, light** and **well drained**.

Direct sow seeds at two-week intervals all spring to prolong the bloom. This plant resents having its roots disturbed. Seeds started indoors should be planted in peat pots or pellets to avoid damaging the roots when the young plants are transferred into the garden.

Tips

This attractive, airy plant is often used in mixed beds and borders. The flowers appear to float above the delicate foliage. The blooming may slow down and the plants may die back if the weather gets too hot for them during the summer.

The stems of this plant can be a bit floppy and may benefit from being staked with twiggy branches. Poke the branches in around the plants while they are young, and the plants will grow up between the twigs.

Recommended

N. damascena forms a loose mound of finely divided foliage. It grows 18–24" tall and spreads about half this much. The light blue flowers darken as they mature. **Miss Jekyll Series** bears semi-double flowers in rose pink, sky blue or a deep cornflower blue that pairs especially well with the golden yellow of *Coreopsis*. Plants in this series grow to about 18" in height. '**Mulberry Rose**' bears light pink flowers that mature to dark pink. **Persian Jewels Series** contains some of the most common cultivars, with plants that grow to about 16" tall and have flowers in purple, rose and white.

N. damascena (photos this page)

Marigold

Tagetes

Height: 7–36" **Spread:** 12–24" **Flower color:** yellow, red, orange, brown, gold, cream, bicolored

FOR EVERY SELF-PROCLAIMED BROWN-THUMB GARDENER, THERE is a marigold ready, willing and waiting to grow. If the common French marigold doesn't satisfy any longer, try the single-flowered signet marigold. The taller varieties, described variously as African or American marigolds, typically have much larger blooms than the French or signet types. The downside is that the African types need to be deadheaded so the fading flowers don't decay and set off a gray mold infection. And beware of the odor of marigold foliage—you can tolerate it but probably will not love it. Choose a planting site carefully.

Planting

Seeding: Start indoors in spring or earlier

Planting out: Once soil has warmed

Spacing: Dwarf marigolds, 6"; tall marigolds, 12"

Growing

Marigolds grow best in **full sun**. The soil should be of **average fertility** and **well drained**. These plants are drought tolerant and hold up well in windy, rainy weather.

Remove spent blooms to encourage more flowers and to keep plants tidy.

Tips

Mass planted or mixed with other plants, marigolds make a vibrant addition to beds, borders and containers gardens. These plants will thrive in the hottest, driest parts of your garden.

T. tenuifolia (above), *T. patula* (below)

When using marigolds as cut flowers, remove the lower leaves to take away some of the pungent scent.

T. erecta with *Rudbeckia, Verbena, Ageratum*

T. tenuifolia *is used as a culinary or tea herb in some Latin American countries, where it is native.*

T. patula

Recommended

T. erecta (African marigold, American marigold, Aztec marigold) is 20–36" tall, with huge yellow to orange flowers. 'Inca' bears double flowers in solid or multi-colored shades of yellow, gold and orange on compact plants that grow to 18" tall. 'Marvel' is another compact cultivar, growing only 18" tall, but with the large flowers that make the species popular. 'Vanilla' bears unique, cream white flowers on compact, odorless plants.

T. patula (French marigold) is low growing, only 7–10" tall. **Bonanza Series** includes popular double-flowered cultivars. The flowers are red, orange, yellow or bicolored. **Hero Series** plants grow only 8–10" tall and bear double flowers, with some bicolors. **Janie Series** includes popular early-blooming, compact plants with red, orange or yellow double blooms. **Safari Series** plants grow 12" tall and have 2$^{1}/_{2}$" wide, double flowers.

T. tenuifolia (signet marigold) has dainty single flowers that grow on bushy plants with lacy foliage. **Gem Series** is commonly available. The compact plants, about 10" tall, bear flowers in shades of yellow and orange, and the edible blooms last all summer.

T. **Triploid Hybrids** (triploid marigold) have been developed by crossing *T. erecta* and *T. patula*. The resulting plants have the huge flowers of African marigold and the compact growth of French marigold. These hybrids are the most heat resistant of all the marigolds. They generally grow about 12" tall and spread 12–24". **'Nugget'** bears large yellow, red, orange, gold or bicolored flowers on low, wide-spreading plants. Plants in the **Zenith Series** have semi-double to double flowers in many yellow, orange or red shades, or bicolors.

T. patula cultivar (above), *T. tenuifolia* (below)

Problems & Pests

Slugs and snails can chew marigold seedlings to the ground. Thrips and mites may develop in mature foliage.

T. erecta *and* T. patula *are often used in vegetable gardens for their reputed insect-repelling qualities.*

Mexican Sunflower

Tithonia

Height: 2–6' **Spread:** 12–24" **Flower color:** orange, red-orange, yellow

MEXICAN SUNFLOWER TAKES ITS TIME COMING INTO ITS PRIME—
sometimes we have to wait until nearly August before the multiple showy
flowers on tall, somewhat gangly stems wave over the garden. But it is by
then that butterfly populations are looking for feeding sources, and Mexican
sunflower can attract more than its share of these glorious insect visitors.

Planting

Seeding: Indoors in early spring; direct sow in spring

Planting out: Once soil has warmed

Spacing: 12–24"

*Don't crowd this plant,
or it may become
susceptible to aphids and
other sucking insects.*

Growing

Mexican sunflower grows best in **full sun**. The soil should be of **average to poor fertility** and **well drained**. Cover seeds lightly; they germinate better when exposed to some light. Mexican sunflower needs little water or care but blooms more profusely if deadheaded regularly.

Tips

Mexican sunflower is heat resistant, so it is ideal for growing in a sunny, dry, warm spot such as under the eaves of a south-facing wall. The plants are tall and break easily if exposed to too much wind; grow along a wall or fence to provide shelter and stability. This coarse annual is well suited to the back of a border, where it will provide a good backdrop to a bed of shorter plants.

Recommended

T. rotundifolia is a vigorous, bushy plant. It grows 3–6' tall and spreads 12–24". Vibrant orange-red flowers are produced from mid- to late summer through to frost. The leaves and stems are covered in a downy fuzz. 'Fiesta del Sol' bears bright orange flowers on plants about 30" tall. 'Goldfinger' grows 24–36" tall and bears large orange flowers. 'Torch' has red-orange flowers. 'Yellow Torch' has bright yellow flowers.

Problems & Pests

This plant is generally resistant to problems; however, young foliage may suffer slug and snail damage. Aphids can become a problem if not dealt with immediately.

T. rotundifolia (above), 'Torch' (below)

For a hot look along a sunny fence or wall, mix Mexican sunflower with other sunflowers and marigolds.

Mignonette
Reseda

Height: 12–24" **Spread:** 6–12" **Flower color:** yellow, reddish-green; plant grown mainly for scent

GROWN IN 18TH-CENTURY EUROPE IN BALCONY planters for its powerful raspberry-vanilla fragrance, mignonette was known as 'Frenchman's darling.' It has made the transition to the 21st century effortlessly. Blend it with showier, unscented flowers in a mixed planting, or try it in a container planting to make its perfume available near a seating area.

Planting

Seeding: Start indoors in late winter or direct sow in mid-spring

Planting out: Around last-frost date

Spacing: About 9"

Growing

Mignonette grows well in **full sun** or **partial shade**. The soil should be of **average fertility, slightly alkaline** and **well drained**. Deadheading will prolong the flowering period.

Tips

Mignonette can be included in a mixed border, preferably near a window, patio or frequently used pathway, so the scent can be enjoyed. Combine mignonette with showier plants for visual as well as olfactory stimulation in the garden or in a bouquet.

This plant attracts bees and other pollen-loving insects to the garden.

Recommended

R. odorata is a bushy, upright plant grown for the long-lasting fragrance of the inconspicuous reddish green flowers. **'Fragrant Beauty'** has red-tinged green flowers and a very sweet fragrance. Some newer cultivars have more decorative flowers but are not as scented.

The genus name Reseda *is from the Latin* resedo, *'to heal' or 'to calm,' referring to the medicinal properties attributed to this plant. The Romans are said to have used it to treat bruises.*

This fragrant annual rarely suffers from any pest or disease problems.

Monkey Flower

Mimulus

Height: 6–12" **Spread:** 12–24" **Flower color:** bright and pastel shades of orange, yellow, burgundy, pink, red, cream or bicolors

VELVETY, TUBULAR FLOWERS THAT ARE THOUGHT TO RESEMBLE grinning monkey faces led to the common name of these plants. A wide range of colors and a floriferous habit should gain them fans. Containers and hanging baskets are a natural; toward the front of a flower border also suits monkey flowers well.

Planting

Seeding: Indoors in early spring

Planting out: Once soil warms after last frost

Spacing: 10–12"

Growing

Monkey flowers prefer **partial or light shade.** Protection from the afternoon sun will prolong the blooming of these plants. The soil should be **fertile, moist** and **humus rich.** Don't allow the soil to dry out. These plants can become scraggly and unattractive in hot sun.

Tips

Monkey flowers make an excellent addition to a border near a pond or to a bog garden. In a flowerbed, border or container garden, they will need to be watered regularly.

These plants are perennials that are grown as annuals. They can be kept over the winter indoors in a cool, bright room.

Recommended

M. x *hybridus* is a group of upright plants with spotted flowers. They grow 6–12" tall and spread 12". '**Calypso**' bears a mixture of flower colors. '**Mystic Mixed**' is compact and early flowering and offers a wide range of bright flower colors in solids or bicolors.

M. luteus (yellow monkey flower), though not as common as the hybrids, is worth growing for its spreading habit and attractive yellow flowers. It grows about 12" tall and spreads up to 24". The yellow flowers are sometimes spotted with red or purple.

Problems & Pests

Downy or powdery mildew, gray mold, whiteflies, spider mites and aphids can cause problems.

M. x *hybridus* 'Mystic Mixed' (photos this page)

These plants tend to fade in summer heat, so they work well in damp, partly shaded spots.

Mimulus, *the genus name for these cheerful flowers, means 'little actor' or 'little mime.'*

Morning Glory

Moonflower, Sweet Potato Vine, Mina Lobata

Ipomoea

Height: 15"–15' **Spread:** 1–15' **Flower color:** white, blue, pink, red, yellow, orange, purple, sometimes bicolored; some types grown for foliage

THESE HEAVY-DUTY FLOWERING VINES ARE GROWN AS ANNUALS in Illinois. Morning glories are ubiquitous, fast-growing, floriferous plants with cup-shaped blooms that attract butterflies and hummingbirds. Moonflower *(I. alba)* is a white-flowered plant that needs warmth to bloom—but when it does, inhale deeply. The possible downside is that its tendrils will clamp onto a hosting support and resent being removed. Sweet potato vine *(I. batatas)* has had a gaga response from the industry and should be grown if you haven't tried it yet.

If 'easy to grow' is your gardening motto, the morning glories are for you.

Planting

Seeding: Indoors in early spring; direct sow after last frost

Planting out: Late spring

Spacing: 12–18"

Growing

Grow these plants in **full sun**. Any type of soil will do, but a **light, well-drained** soil of **poor to average fertility** is preferred. *I. alba* needs warm weather to bloom.

These plants must twine around objects in order to climb them. Wide fence posts, walls or other broad objects must have a trellis or some wire or twine attached to provide the vines something to grow on.

Soak seeds for 24 hours before sowing. If starting seeds indoors, plant them in individual peat pots.

Tips

These vines can be grown anywhere: fences, walls, trees, trellises and arbors are all possible supports. As groundcovers, morning glories will grow over any obstacles they encounter. They can also be grown in hanging baskets.

If you have a bright sunny window, consider starting a hanging basket of morning glories indoors for a unique winter display. The vines will twine around the hangers and spill over the sides of the pot, providing you with beautiful trumpet flowers, regardless of the weather outside.

Each flower of a morning glory plant lasts only one day. The buds form a spiral that slowly unfurls as the day brightens with the rising sun.

I. tricolor

Grow moonflower on a trellis near a porch or patio that is used in the evenings, so that the sweetly scented flowers can be fully enjoyed. Once evening falls, the huge, white blossoms pour forth their sweet nectar, attracting night-flying moths.

I. batatas 'Tricolor' (above),
'Blackie' with annuals (below)

Recommended

I. alba (moonflower) has sweet-scented, white flowers that open only at night. It grows up to 15' tall.

I. batatas (sweet potato vine) is a twining climber that is grown for its attractive foliage rather than its flowers. Often used in planters and hanging baskets, sweet potato vine can be used by itself or mixed with other plants. It may spread or climb 10' or more in a summer. As a bonus, when you pull up your plant at the end of summer, you can eat the enlarged tuber-like roots (sweet potatoes). **'Black Heart'** is more compact than the species. It has heart-shaped, dark purple-green foliage with darker veins. **'Blackie'** has dark purple (almost black), deeply lobed leaves. **'Margarita'** has yellow-green foliage and fairly compact growth. This cascading plant can also be trained to grow up a trellis. **'Tricolor'** has foliage variegated

pink, green and white. It is not as vigorous as the others, growing to only 15".

I. lobata (mina lobata, firecracker vine, exotic love) is a twining climber 6–15' tall. The flowers are borne along one side of a spike. The buds are red and the flowers mature to orange then yellow, giving the spike a fire-like appearance.

I. tricolor (morning glory) is a twining climber that can grow 10–12' tall in a single summer. There are many cultivars of this species available, although some listed as such may actually be cultivars of *I. nil.* '**Blue Star**' bears blue-and-white-streaked flowers. '**Heavenly Blue**' bears sky blue flowers with a white center.

Problems & Pests

Morning glories are susceptible to several fungal problems, but they occur only rarely.

Sweet potato vine is often recognized by its large, lime green, heart-shaped leaves, but the foliage is also available in purple. Unlike the more aggressive morning glory species, sweet potato vine doesn't twine or grasp or get carried away. It drapes politely over the sides of containers or spreads neatly beneath taller plants.

I. batatas 'Margarita' (above) & with *Petunia* & *Zinnia* (below)

Musk Mallow

Abelmoschus

Height: 18"– 5' **Spread:** 18–24" **Flower color:** white to yellow with purple centers, red with white centers, pink, orange

MOST ANNUAL VARIETIES OF MUSK MALLOW ARE DERIVED FROM *A. moschatus*, with wonderful flowers that resemble hibiscus. The 'musk' part of the common name refers to the seedpod of *A. moschatus*, which has a smell not everyone finds appealing. The very similar pod in another member of this genus *(A. esculentus)* is the okra of gumbo fame. Watch for new cultivars of *A. esculentus* being introduced under the name ornamental okra.

Abelmoschus *is from the Arabic* abulmosk, *'father of musk,' and like the common name refers to the musk-scented seeds.*

Planting

Seeding: Sow seed indoors in late winter or early spring; direct sow in spring after danger of frost has passed

Planting out: Well after the last frost

Spacing: 12–18"

Growing

Musk mallows prefer **full sun**. The soil should be **fertile** and **well drained**. Fertilize monthly for good performance.

Tips

Use musk mallows in an annual or mixed border. The taller types can be used at the back of the border and the lower cultivars in the middle or near the front.

Recommended

A. esculentus (okra) grows 2–5' tall and 24" wide, with stout stems. The flowers are white to bright yellow with purple or red in the center. 'Burgundy' grows 4' tall and produces burgundy-tinged green leaves and burgundy seedpods.

A. moschatus (musk mallow) is a bushy perennial that is grown as an annual in cold winter climates. The flowers can be up to 4" across. The seeds have a musky scent. **'Oriental Red'** bears red flowers that fade to white at the centers. **Pacific Series** has compact plants that grow to 18" tall, with flowers in various colors.

Problems & Pests

Musk mallows may have trouble with fungal diseases, such as powdery mildew and root rot, and with spider mites, slugs and whiteflies.

These plants are related to hibiscus, mallow and hollyhock.

Musk mallow flowers are a poor choice for arrangements because the flowers fade within hours of being cut.

Nasturtium

Tropaeolum

Height: 8–18" for dwarf varieties; up to 10' for trailing varieties
Spread: equal to or slightly greater than height **Flower color:** red, orange, yellow, burgundy, pink, cream, gold, white or bicolored

THERE AREN'T MANY PLANTS THAT WILL LEND BOTH THEIR LEAVES and blooms to a salad, but nasturtium is one such plant. The leaves have a slightly more peppery bite than the flowers. In the flower garden, nasturtium has a reputation as a can't-fail ornamental, but fail it can. About the time spring transplants start to flourish, hot weather arrives and nasturtium may struggle. If your plants start to flag, keep them well watered during the summer heat.

Planting

Seeding: Indoors in late winter; direct sow around last-frost date

Planting out: After last frost

Spacing: 12"

Growing

Nasturtium prefers **full sun** but tolerates some shade. The soil should be of **average to poor fertility, light, moist** and **well drained.** Too rich a soil or too much nitrogen fertilizer will result in lots of leaves and very few flowers. Let the soil drain completely between waterings.

If you start nasturtium seeds indoors, sow them in individual peat pots to avoid disturbing the roots during transplanting.

Alaska Series (above), *T. majus* & lettuce (below)

The painter Claude Monet was a fan of nasturtium, lining the entryway to his home in the south of France with this colorful and edible ornamental.

T. majus (above), Alaska Series (below)

Tips

Nasturtium can be used in beds and borders, in containers and hanging baskets and on sloped banks. The climbing varieties are grown up trellises or over rock walls or places that need concealing. This plant thrives in poor locations, and it makes an interesting addition to plantings on hard-to-mow slopes.

Some gardeners believe that nasturtium attracts and harbors certain pests, such as whiteflies and aphids, and that it should not be grown near plants that are susceptible to the same problems. Other gardeners believe that nasturtium is preferred by pest insects and that the pests will flock to it and leave the rest of the garden alone. Still other gardeners claim that this plant, because of the high sulfur levels in the leaves, repels many pests that would otherwise infest the garden. Whatever the case, if you do find aphids on your nasturtiums, you will notice that they congregate near the growing tips. Cut the infested parts off and drop them in a bucket of soapy water to rid yourself of this problem.

Recommended

T. majus has a trailing habit. It has been greatly improved by hybridizing. The foliage of the older varieties tended to hide the flowers, but new varieties hold their flowers—available in a great selection of colors—above the foliage. There are also some new and interesting cultivars with variegated foliage and compact, attractive, mound-forming habits. **Alaska Series** plants have white-marbled foliage. **'Empress of India'** grows 8–12" tall and 12–18" wide, with deep crimson flowers and dark purple-blue foliage. **Jewel Series** includes compact plants that grow to 12" tall and wide, with double flowers in a mix of deep orange, red or gold. **'Peach Melba'** forms a 12" mound. The flowers are pale yellow with a bright orange-red splash at the base of each petal. **'Whirlybird'** is a compact, bushy plant. The single or double flowers in shades of red, pink, yellow or orange do not have spurs.

Problems & Pests

The few problems that afflict nasturtium include aphids, slugs, whiteflies and some viruses.

Nasturtium has a place in any vegetable or herb garden. The leaves and flowers are edible and can be added to salads, soups and dips. They have a peppery flavor, so don't overdo it. The unripe seedpods can be pickled and used as a substitute for capers (see recipe).

'Peach Melba' (above), Alaska Series (below)

RECIPE

Poor Man's Capers (Pickled Nasturtium Seedpods)

Soak green seedpods for 24 hours in a brine made from 2 cups of water and 1 tbsp. salt.

Pack small, sterilized jars with the drained seedpods. Include one peeled clove of garlic and 1 tsp. pickling spices in each jar.

Heat white wine vinegar to simmering and fill each jar with the vinegar.

Seal with acid-proof lids and let the seedpods sit for about a month.

The pickled seedpods should be eaten within a week of opening.

Nemesia

Nemesia

Height: 8–24" **Spread:** 4–12" **Flower color:** blue, purple, pink, white

NEMESIA'S CLUSTERS OF MINIATURE SNAPDRAGON-LIKE FLOWERS bloom atop branched stems with narrow, bright green leaves. Two or more colors may appear in a single flower. Nemesia is ideal as an edging plant and for hanging baskets, window boxes and mixed borders. It is another in the group of annuals that would really rather the temperature never surpass 70° F. Breeders are, however, developing more heat-tolerant varieties.

Planting

Seeding: Start indoors in early spring

Planting out: After last frost

Spacing: 6"

Growing

Nemesia prefers **full sun**. The soil should be **average to fertile, slightly acidic, moist** and **well drained**. Regular watering will keep this plant blooming through the summer.

Tips

Nemesia makes a bright and colorful addition to the front of a mixed border or mixed container planting.

Recommended

N. caerulea (N. fruticans) is a bushy plant that grows up to 24" tall and spreads about 12". It bears blue, pink, purple or white flowers. Several cultivars are available as transplants. **'Blue Bird'** bears lavender blue flowers on plants 8–12" tall. **'Blue Lagoon'** also grows 8–12" tall, producing slate blue flowers. **'Candy Girl'** bears frilled, fragrant, light pink flowers on 10–12" tall plants. **'Compact Innocence'** grows 10–12" tall, and **'Innocence'** grows 12–14" tall; both have fragrant, lilac-scented white flowers. The preceding cultivars can all be planted out in early spring and will tolerate frosts and cool temperatures, but they are also very heat tolerant when fertilized regularly. **Safari Series** includes vigorous plants growing 8–14" tall, with good heat tolerance and fragrant blooms. In this series, **'Pink'** has pink flowers, and **'Plum'** features large purple flowers.

Problems & Pests

Occasional problems with crown or root rot are possible.

Passion Flower

Passiflora

Height: up to 30' **Spread:** variable **Flower color:** white or pale pink petals with blue or purple bands

MANY BIBLICAL REFERENCES ARE ASSOCIATED WITH THE COMMON name of this truly exotic vine. The blooms are spectacular, sometimes coming in bicolors or tricolors. If you have a bright enough space indoors, bring these plants inside for the winter—they are great conservatory plants.

Planting

Seeding: Not recommended

Planting out: Several weeks after last frost

Spacing: 12"

The common name refers not to physical love but to Christ's Passion. The three stigmas of the flower are said to represent the nails and the five anthers the wounds.

Growing

Grow passion flower in **full sun** or **partial shade**. This plant prefers **well-drained, moist** soil of **average fertility**. Keep it **sheltered** from wind and cold.

Germination is erratic and propagation is generally easier from cuttings. Gardeners who like a challenge can try growing passion flower from seed. Soak seeds for 24 hours in hot water before planting. Place the seed tray in full sun because the seeds need light to germinate. Keep the soil moist and at about 59° F.

P. caerulea (photos this page)

Fertilize passion flower sparingly. Too much nitrogen will encourage lots of foliage but few flowers.

Tips

Passion flower is a popular addition to mixed containers and makes an unusual focal point near a door or other entryway. This plant is actually a fast-growing woody climber that is grown as an annual.

Many garden centers now sell small passion flower plants in spring. They quickly climb trellises and other supports over summer. They can be composted at the end of summer or cut back and brought inside to enjoy in a bright room over winter.

The small round fruits are edible but not very tasty.

Recommended

P. caerulea (blue passion flower) bears unusual purple-banded, purple-white flowers all summer. 'Constance Elliott' ('Constance Eliott') has fragrant white flowers.

Problems & Pests

Spider mites, whiteflies, scale insects and nematodes may cause trouble.

Persian Shield

Strobilanthes

Height: 18–36" **Spread:** 24–36" **Flower color:** blue; plant grown for green, purple and silver foliage

'IRIDESCENT' IS A STRONG WORD TO USE FOR A PLANT, BUT IT'S used appropriately when trying to describe the grayish purple foliage of Persian shield. Although this plant is shrubby, it tends to tip over, and it looks best as a groundcover in a flowerbed or as a draping accent in a container situation. The inconspicuous flowers often don't form before frost.

Take stem-tip cuttings in late summer and plant them in pots to color up your indoor garden over the winter.

Planting

Seeding: Not recommended

Planting out: In warm soil after last frost

Spacing: 24"

Growing

Persian shield grows well in **partial to full shade**. Keep it out of the hot midday sun. A spot that receives morning sun but afternoon shade is good. The soil should be **average to fertile, light** and very **well drained**. Do not allow the soil to dry completely. Pinch growing tips to encourage bushiness.

Tips

The colorful foliage provides a dramatic background in annual or mixed borders and in container plantings. Combine with yellow or white flowers for a stunning contrast.

Recommended

S. dyerianus is a tender shrub that is grown as an annual. It forms a bushy mound of silver- or purple-flushed foliage with contrasting dark green or purple veins and margins. The foliage emerges purple and matures to silver. Plants may produce spikes of blue flowers in early fall.

Problems & Pests

Trouble with root rot is possible in very wet soils.

The common name arose because this plant's foliage was thought to resemble the colorful shields carried by soldiers in ancient Persia.

Petunia

Petunia

Height: 6–18" **Spread:** 12–24" or more **Flower color:** pink, purple, red, white, yellow, coral, blue or bicolored

PETUNIAS MIGHT NOT TAKE UP EVERY SQUARE INCH OF YOUR flowerbeds the way they might once have, but with many exciting new types and improved traditional varieties coming on the market, petunias have never been better. Look especially for three types at the garden center: Waves, Supertunias and Surfinias. Species petunias are known for their fragrance, and even from the hybrids you'll be able to get a distinct sweet whiff toward evening.

Planting

Seeding: Indoors in mid-winter

Planting out: After last frost

Spacing: 12–18"

Growing

Petunias prefer **full sun**. The soil should be of **average to rich fertility, light, sandy** and **well drained**. When sowing, press seeds into the soil surface but don't cover them with soil. Pinch halfway back in mid-summer to keep plants bushy and to encourage new growth and flowers.

Tips

Use petunias in beds, borders, containers and hanging baskets.

Recommended

P. x *hybrida* is a large group of popular, sun-loving annuals that fall into three categories: grandifloras, multifloras and millifloras.

The **grandiflora** petunias have the largest flowers—up to 4" across. They have the widest variety of colors and forms, but they are the most likely to be damaged by heavy rain. **Daddy Series** is available in darkly veined shades of pink and purple. **Supercascade Series** comes in a wide variety of colors. **Ultra Series** is available in many colors, including bicolors, and these cultivars recover quite quickly from weather damage.

Compared to the grandifloras, the **multiflora** petunias have smaller blooms (about half the size), bear many more flowers and tolerate adverse weather conditions better. **Carpet Series** is available in a wide variety of colors. Petunias in the

Grandiflora type (above), Fantasy Series (below)

With the introduction of many wonderful new varieties, petunias may again outrank impatiens as America's most popular bedding plants.

Grandiflora type (above), 'Lavender Wave' (below)

Surfinia Series branch freely, are self-cleaning and form a neat mound covered by a mass of flowers in shades of pink, blue, purple and white. Look for new additions to the series, which feature double flowers, minis, pastel colors and decorative veining. **Wave Series** plants have flowers in pink, purple or coral. The low, spreading habit makes this series popular as groundcovers and for hanging baskets and containers. The plants recover well from rain damage, bloom nonstop, tolerate cold and spread quickly.

The **milliflora** petunias are the newest group. The flowers are about 1" across and are borne profusely over the whole plant. These plants tolerate wet weather very well and sometimes self-seed. They are popular in mixed containers and hanging baskets and are also very nice in garden beds, forming neat mounds of foliage and flowers. **Fantasy Series** is

available in shades of red, purple, pink and white, although the pinks tend to be easiest to find. **Supertunia Mini Series** varieties bear small, weather-resistant blue, pink, lilac, purple or white flowers on well-branched plants. Some of the flowers in this series have darkened veins on the petals. With the growing popularity of the millifloras, more colors will very likely become available.

Problems & Pests

Aphids and fungi may present problems. Fungal problems can be avoided by wetting the foliage as little as possible and by providing a location with good drainage.

The name Petunia *is derived from* petun, *the Brazilian word for tobacco, which comes from species of the related genus* Nicotiana.

Milliflora type (above), 'Blue Wave' (below)

Phlox

Phlox

Height: 6–18" **Spread:** 10" or more **Flower color:** purple, pink, red, blue, white, yellow

ANNUAL PHLOX IS THE LOW-GROWING, LONG-FLOWERING COUSIN of the popular perennial. You will see it growing wild along highways. Its showy, tubular flowers can be a wide range of colors, usually with a lighter 'eye' in the center. The flowers, like the leaves and stems, are covered with glandular hairs. Annual phlox looks good in a mixed spring planter, makes a good cut flower and attracts hummingbirds. If your early-season blooms give way to summer heat, try reseeding for a show in the cooler days of autumn.

This Texan species of phlox is named for Thomas Drummond (1790–1835), who collected plants in North America.

Planting

Seeding: Direct sow in early spring and mid-summer

Spacing: Up to 8"

Growing

Phlox prefers **full sun**. The soil should be **fertile, moist** and **well drained**. This plant resents being transplanted, and starting it indoors is not recommended. Germination takes 10–15 days. Phlox can be propagated from cuttings and will root easily in moist soil. Plants can be spaced quite close together.

Deadhead to promote blooming.

Tips

Use phlox on rock walls and in beds, borders, containers and rock gardens.

Recommended

P. drummondii forms a bushy plant 6–18" tall and 10" or more in spread. It can be upright or spreading, and it bears clusters of white, purple, pink or red flowers. '**Coral Reef**' bears attractive pastel-colored flowers. **Twinkle Mix** includes compact plants 8" tall, with unusual small, star-shaped flowers. The colors of the petal margins and centers often contrast with the main petal color.

Problems & Pests

To avoid fungal problems, provide good drainage and don't let water stand on the leaves late in the day. Water the plants in the morning during dry spells and avoid handling wet foliage.

P. drummondii (photos this page)

Start phlox seed again in mid-summer to enjoy late-summer and fall blooms.

Pincushion Flower
Scabiosa
Scabiosa

Height: 18–36" **Spread:** up to 12" **Flower color:** purple, blue, maroon, pink, white, red

THE ANNUAL PINCUSHION FLOWERS HAVE THE SAME fully double blooms as the perennial species but come in more colors. Most varieties are fragrant. The cultivar 'Ace of Spades' has nearly black blooms; several other varieties have deep purple to deep red flower stalks. Pincushion flowers will blend well into any wildflower or cottage garden.

Planting

Seeding: Indoors in late winter; direct sow in mid-spring

Planting out: After last frost

Spacing: 12–16"

Growing

Pincushion flowers grow best in **full sun**. The soil should be of **average to rich fertility, alkaline, well drained** and rich in **organic matter**. Keep the soil moderately moist, but do not overwater.

Tips

Pincushion flowers are useful in beds, borders and mixed containers. The flowers are also popular in fresh arrangements.

The tall stems of *S. atropurpurea* may fall over as the plants mature. Insert twiggy branches, called pea sticks, into the ground around the plants when they are small to give them support as they grow.

Recommended

S. atropurpurea is an upright, branching plant growing up to 36" tall and spreading about 12". The species has purple or crimson flowers; cultivars can come in white or blue as well. **'Ace of Spades'** has deep maroon flowers with a honey scent; it grows to 24" tall. **'Imperial Giants'** bears blooms in a deep maroon as well as shades of pink.

S. stellata grows 18" tall and spreads half as much. This plant bears small white flowers but is grown for its papery, orb-like seedpods, which dry in unusual globe shapes and are useful accents in dried arrangements. Pick *S. stellata* while still slightly green to keep the dried seedpods from shattering. **'Drumstick'** ('Paper Moon') bears blue flowers. The seedpods dry to a warm bronze color.

S. atropurpurea

The name Scabiosa *is related to 'scabies,' which the plant was once thought to cure.*

The rounded, densely petaled blooms serve as a perfect landing pad for butterflies.

S. atropurpurea 'Imperial Giants'

Polka Dot Plant

Hypoestes

Height: 12–24" **Spread:** 8–12" **Flower color:** purple, inconspicuous; plant grown for pink-, red- or white-spotted leaves

DAPPLED FOLIAGE IS THE HIGHLIGHT OF THIS PLANT. ITS LEAVES appear to have been spattered with paint in colors of white through reddish. Although it is recommended for sunny locations, I have often seen it best used to brighten a light-shade location. Often sold as a houseplant, polka dot plant can also be added to containers. The trick is to make the plants bushy—pinch out top growth to keep them low and full.

Planting

Seeding: Indoors in early spring

Planting out: After last-frost date

Spacing: 12"

Growing

Polka dot plant prefers **full sun** but tolerates light shade. Too much shade will reduce leaf coloration and can encourage floppy growth. The soil should be of **average fertility, humus rich, moist** and **well drained**.

Pinch growing tips frequently to encourage bushy growth. Pinch off the inconspicuous flowers or the plants may decline.

Tips

Polka dot plant can be used in small groups as accent plants, in mass plantings and in mixed containers. In general it looks best when at least a few of the plants are used in a group rather than single plants spaced farther apart.

Recommended

H. phyllostachya (*H. sanguinolenta*) is a bushy plant grown for its attractive foliage. This species has mostly green leaves that are lightly dusted with pink spots. Several cultivars have been developed with more dramatic foliage. **Confetti Series** has foliage that is heavily spotted light or dark pink or white. **Splash Series** has foliage that is brightly streaked and spotted with pink, white or red.

Problems & Pests

This plant is usually problem free, but rare instances of powdery mildew can occur.

Splash Series

Polka dot plant is often grown as a houseplant, doing best in a sunny window.

Confetti Series

Poppy
Papaver

Height: 1–4' **Spread:** 8–12" **Flower color:** red, pink, white, purple, yellow, orange

HERE'S A GROUP OF ANNUALS WITH AN UNUSUAL GROWING CYCLE. It is recommended that you plant poppies in fall and plan to dig them out in early summer, by which time they have probably left seedlings behind to bring you new poppies the following spring. The nodding heads and papery petals, along with the characteristic bright colors, make these plants popular. They grow reliably no matter how you treat them.

These fleeting beauties will not interfere with later-blooming perennials. Simply remove the spent poppies as they decline.

Planting

Seeding: Direct sow every two weeks in spring

Spacing: 12"

Growing

Poppies grow best in **full sun**. The soil should be **fertile** and **sandy** and have lots of **organic matter** mixed in. **Good drainage** is essential. Do not start seeds indoors because transplanting is often unsuccessful. Mix the tiny seeds with fine sand for even sowing. Do not cover, because the seeds need light to germinate. Deadhead to prolong blooming.

Tips

Poppies work well in mixed borders where other plants are slow to fill in. The poppies will fill in empty spaces early in the season then die back over the summer, leaving room for other plants. They can also be used in rock gardens, and the cut flowers are popular for fresh arrangements.

Be careful when weeding around faded summer plants; you may accidentally pull up germinating poppy seedlings.

The large seed capsules of opium poppy can be dried and used in floral arrangements.

Recommended

P. nudicaule (Iceland poppy) is a short-lived perennial that is grown as an annual. It grows 12–18" tall and spreads about 12". Red, orange, yellow, pink or white flowers appear in spring and early summer. This plant tends to self-seed, but it will gradually disappear from the garden

P. nudicaule (photos this page)

Use of poppy seeds in cooking and baking can be traced as far back as the ancient Egyptians.

P. rupifragum (above),
P. somniferum 'Peony Flowered' (below)

if it is left to its own devices.
'**Champagne Bubbles**' bears 3" wide flowers in solid and bicolored shades of red, orange and yellow.

P. rhoeas (Flanders poppy, field poppy, corn poppy) forms a basal rosette of foliage above which the flowers are borne on long stems. '**Mother of Pearl**' bears flowers in pastel pinks and purples. **Shirley Series** (Shirley poppy) has silky, cup-shaped petals. The flowers come in many colors and may be single, semi-double or double.

P. rupifragum (apricota poppy) is a perennial from Spain that can be grown as an annual. It grows 18" tall and 8–10" wide and produces pale brick red flowers over a long period in summer.

P. somniferum (opium poppy) grows up to 4' tall. The flowers are red, pink, white or purple. This plant has a mixed reputation. Its milky sap is the source of several drugs, including codeine, morphine and opium. All parts of the plant can cause stomach upset and even coma except for the seeds, which are a popular culinary additive (poppy seeds). The seeds contain only minute amounts of the chemicals that make this plant pharmaceutically valuable. Though propagation of the species is restricted in many countries, several attractive cultivars have been developed for ornamental use. '**Danebrog Lace**' originated in the 19th century. The single flowers have frilly red petals with a large white patch at the base of each petal. '**Hens 'n' Chicks**' bears large flowers and large, decorative seedheads.

Each large seedhead is surrounded by numerous smaller seedheads, like a mother hen surrounded by her chicks. **'Peony Flowered'** has large, frilly double flowers in a variety of colors on plants that grow up to 36" in height.

Problems & Pests

Poppies rarely have problems, although fungi may be troublesome if the soil is wet and poorly drained.

P. somniferum 'Hens 'n' Chicks'

For cut flowers, seal the cut end of each stem with a flame or boiling water.

P. rhoeas Shirley Series

Portulaca
Moss Rose
Portulaca

Height: 4–8" **Spread:** 6–12" or more **Flower color:** red, pink, yellow, white, purple, orange, peach

THE REIGNING CHAMPIONS OF THE BRIGHTEST SPOTS IN THE garden have to be the portulacas. They love the heat, flower all season, stay in bounds (at least height-wise) and generally don't fuss if you forget to water them. The succulent foliage gives the plants a different texture than that of many of their annual compatriots.

Planting
Seeding: Indoors in late winter

Planting out: Once soil has warmed

Spacing: 12"

Growing

Portulacas require **full sun**. The soil should be of **poor fertility, sandy** and **well drained**. To ensure that you will have plants where you want them, start seed indoors. If you sow directly outdoors, the tiny seeds may get washed away by rain and the plants will pop up in unexpected places. Spacing the plants close together is not a problem; in fact, it results in well-mixed flower colors.

Tips

Portulacas are the ideal plants for spots that just don't get enough water—under the eaves of the house or in dry, rocky, exposed areas. They are also ideal for people who like baskets hanging from the front porch but always forget to water them. As long as the location is sunny, these plants will do well with minimal care.

Recommended

P. grandiflora forms a bushy mound of succulent foliage. It bears delicate, papery, rose-like flowers profusely all summer. **'Cloudbeater'** bears large double flowers in many colors. The flowers stay open all day, even in cloudy weather. **Margarita Series** plants have semi-double flowers in white, cream, yellow, orange, pink and red. All-America Selections winner 'Margarita Rosita' has deep pink flowers. **Sundial Series** plants have long-lasting double flowers. AAS winner 'Sundial Peach' has double flowers in shades of peach.

P. oleracea **Duet Series** is a group of low-growing plants that work best in

With only minimal attention, portulacas will fill a sunny, exposed strip of soil next to pavement with bright colors all summer.

P. grandiflora

baskets, where they can trail over the edges. The single flowers are large and bicolored. **'Candy Stripe'** is a cultivar in the series with white flowers that have red margins.

Problems & Pests

If portulacas have excellent drainage and as much light as possible, they shouldn't have problems.

Rose-of-Heaven
Silene, Campion, Catchfly
Silene

Height: 6–24" **Spread:** 6" **Flower color:** pink, white, blue

WE ALL STRIVE TO PUT AT LEAST ONE SPECIMEN OF AN exotic nature in our gardens each year, and rose-of-heaven is a good candidate for the role. Typically grown in England and Europe, these plants are available in Illinois if you look hard enough. The farther south you are in the state, the more challenging it becomes to find them because they prefer cooler climates. Try growing a rose-of-heaven as a biennial, and see if it returns after the first summer to bloom in cooler days the following spring.

The stems of some species are sticky and can trap small insects, hence the alternative common name catchfly.

Planting

Seeding: Direct sow around last-frost date or seed indoors in mid-spring

Planting out: After last-frost date

Spacing: 6"

Growing

Rose-of-heaven plants grow equally well in **full sun** or **light shade**. The soil should be **fertile, moist** and **well drained**.

Tips

These annuals make good fillers in a shrub or mixed border. They can be included in beds, borders, planters and rock gardens. You may find rose-of-heaven turning up in your garden year after year because the plants tend to self-seed.

Recommended

S. armeria (sweet william catchfly) forms a basal rosette of leaves from which many sticky stems emerge. It grows about 12–24" tall, spreads 6–12" and bears clusters of vivid pink flowers. **'Electra'** bears more flower clusters than the species.

S. coeli-rosa forms an upright plant up to 20" tall and about 6" wide, with slender gray-green leaves. The flowers are bright pink with paler, often white centers. Plants in the **Angel Series** grow 6–20" tall and spread to 6". 'Angel Blue' bears blue flowers. 'Angel Rose' bears bright pink flowers.

S. pendula (nodding catchfly) is a bushy upright or spreading plant. It grows 6–12" tall, with an equal spread, and bears loose clusters of

S. armeria 'Electra'

nodding single or double light pink flowers. **'Peach Blossom'** has flowers that open a deep pink and gradually fade to white as they mature, with flowers in different stages of coloration showing at once. **'Snowball'** bears double white flowers.

Problems & Pests

Aphids, snails, slugs, whiteflies, rust, leaf fungus and spider mites can be problems.

S. pendula 'Peach Blossom'

Salvia
Sage
Salvia

Height: 1–4' **Spread:** 8"–4' **Flower color:** red, blue, purple, burgundy, pink, orange, salmon, yellow, cream, white or bicolored

DESPITE THE PINKS, CORALS AND NUMEROUS OTHER COLORS salvias now come in, for me these plants are most strongly associated with the color blue. I refer to the deep, purplish, intense blue as in 'Victoria,' the most often seen cultivar. Other people may find that red always comes to mind when they think of salvias. Whatever the color, don't overlook the aromatic aspect of these plants—they are sages, after all.

The long-lasting flowers of salvias hold up well in adverse weather.

Planting

Seeding: Indoors in mid-winter; direct sow in spring

Planting out: After last frost

Spacing: 10"

Growing

All salvias prefer **full sun** but tolerate light shade. The soil should be **moist, well drained** and of **average to rich fertility,** with lots of **organic matter.**

To keep plants producing flowers, water often and fertilize monthly. Remove spent flowers before they begin to turn brown.

Tips

Salvias look good grouped in beds, borders and containers. The blooms are long lasting and make lovely cut flowers for arrangements.

S. elegans (above), *S. farinacea* & *S. splendens* (below)

Recommended

S. argentea (silver sage) is grown for its large, fuzzy, silvery leaves. It grows up to 36" tall, spreads about 24" and bears small white or pink-tinged flowers. This plant is a biennial or short-lived perennial grown as an annual.

S. coccinea (bloody sage, Texas sage) grows 24–30" tall and 12" wide and bears dark pink flowers. '**Coral Nymph**' grows 12–20" tall and has bicolored salmon and white flowers. '**Forest Fire**' has red flowers tinged with black on well-branched plants 12–24" tall. '**Lady in Red**,' an All-America Selections winner, grows 12–18" tall and bears scarlet, trumpet-shaped blooms in rings around the flower spike.

S. splendens

S. elegans (S. rutilans; pineapple sage) is a large, bushy plant with soft leaves and bright red flowers. It grows 3–4' tall, with an equal spread. The foliage smells of pineapple when crushed and is used as a culinary flavoring.

S. farinacea (mealy cup sage, blue sage) has bright blue flowers clustered along stems powdered with silver. The plant grows up to 24" tall, with a spread of 12". The flowers are also available in white. '**Victoria**' is a popular cultivar with silvery foliage and deep blue flowers that make a beautiful addition to cut-flower arrangements.

S. patens (gentian sage) bears vivid blue flowers on plants 18–24" tall. This is a tender perennial grown as an annual. Being tuberous-rooted, it can be lifted and brought inside for the winter in the same way as dahlias. '**Cambridge Blue**' bears pale blue flowers.

S. splendens (salvia, scarlet sage) grows 12–18" tall and spreads up to 12". It is known for its spikes of bright red, tubular flowers. Recently, cultivars have become available in white, pink, purple and orange. '**Phoenix**' forms a neat, compact plant with flowers in many bright and pastel shades. '**Salsa**' bears solid or bicolored flowers in shades of red, orange, purple, burgundy, cream or pink. **Sizzler Series** includes plants with flowers in burgundy, lavender, pink, plum, red, salmon, or white and salmon bicolor. '**Vista**' is an early-flowering, compact plant with dark blue-green foliage and bright red flowers.

S. viridis (*S. horminum;* annual clary sage) is grown for its colorful bracts (modified leaves). It grows 18–24" tall, with a spread of 8–12". **'Claryssa'** grows 18" tall and has bracts in pink, purple, blue or white. **'Oxford Blue'** bears purple-blue bracts.

Problems & Pests

Seedlings are prone to damping-off. Aphids and a few fungal problems may trouble adult plants.

The genus name Salvia *comes from the Latin* salvus, *'save,' referring to the medicinal properties of several species.*

S. coccinea 'Coral Nymph' (above),
S. farinacea 'Victoria' (below)

Snapdragon
Antirrhinum

Height: 6"–4' **Spread:** 6–24" **Flower color:** white, cream, yellow, orange, red, maroon, pink, purple, bronze or bicolored

THE NOVELTY OF FINDING JUST THE RIGHT PLACE on a snapdragon bloom to pop open its 'jaws' may wear off after a while. But with their unique floral shapes, their upright stalks that support ever-opening blossoms, and their wide-ranging color selections, snapdragons have remained annual favorites. Breeding has brought out more compact plants, some to under 12" in height. If you're a snapdragon purist, you may find these varieties rather misshapen. Other gardeners will revel in the new range of choices.

Planting
Seeding: Indoors in late winter; direct sow in spring

Planting out: After last frost

Spacing: 6–18"

These plants may self-sow, but the hybrids will not come true to type. Unless you enjoy experimenting, you might wish to pull them out.

Growing

Snapdragons prefer **full sun** but tolerate light or partial shade. The soil should be **fertile,** rich in **organic matter** and **well drained**. Snapdragons prefer a **neutral or alkaline** soil and will not perform as well in acidic soil. Do not cover seeds when sowing because they require light for germination.

To encourage bushier growth, pinch the tips of the plants while they are young. Cut off the flower spikes as they fade to promote further blooming and to prevent the plant from dying back before the end of the season.

Tips

The height of the variety dictates the best place for it in a border—the shortest varieties work well near the front, and the tallest look good in the center or back. The dwarf and medium-height varieties can also be used in planters, and the trailing varieties do well in hanging baskets.

Snapdragons are perennials grown as annuals. They can tolerate cold nights well into fall and may survive a mild winter. Self-sowed seedlings may sprout the following spring if plants are left in place over winter, but because most snapdragons are hybrids they will not come true.

Snapdragons can handle cold weather, so they are a good choice for gardeners who can't wait until the last-frost date to plant their annuals.

Recommended

Many cultivars of *A. majus* are available. Snapdragons are grouped into four classes: dwarf, medium, giant and trailing.

Dwarf varieties grow up to 12" tall. **Tahiti Series** plants are compact, resist rust and bloom in red, orange, rose pink, bronze, or pink and white bicolor.

Medium snapdragons grow 12–24" tall. 'Crown Candycorn' grows to 14" tall and bears red and yellow bicolored flowers. 'Jamaican Mist' bears open, trumpet-shaped flowers in cinnamon, shell pink, yellow, apricot, rose or peach on plants up to 15" tall. **Ribbon Series** plants reach 18–24" in height. These early-blooming cultivars include 'Crimson,' 'Lavender,' 'Light Pink,' 'Purple,' 'Rose,' 'White,' 'Yellow' and a mix of the seven different colors. **Sonnet Series** plants grow to 36" in height and are as attractive as cut flowers as they are in the garden.

Giant or **tall** cultivars can grow 3–4' tall. 'Madame Butterfly' bears double flowers in a wide range of colors. The flowers of this cultivar are open-faced with a ruffled edge and they don't 'snap,' because the hinged, mouth-like structure has been lost with the addition of the extra petals. Plants in the **Rocket Series** produce long spikes of brightly colored flowers in many shades. They have good heat tolerance.

Trailing snapdragons are excellent for containers and hanging baskets. Plants in the **Luminaire Series** from Ball Seed are vigorous and well branched, reaching 12" in height and

16–20" in spread when grown in a 10" diameter container. The series includes 'Bronze and Yellow,' 'Deep Purple,' 'Deep Yellow,' 'Hot Pink,' 'Orange and Yellow,' 'Pink and White' and 'Yellow.'

Problems & Pests

Snapdragons can suffer from several fungal problems, including powdery and downy mildew, fungal leaf spot, root rot and wilt. Snapdragon rust is the worst. To prevent rust, avoid wetting the foliage, choose varieties that are rust resistant and plant snapdragons in different parts of the garden each year. Aphids may also be troublesome.

Snapdragons are interesting and long lasting in fresh flower arrangements. The buds will continue to mature and open even after the spike is cut from the plant.

Spider Flower
Cleome

Height: 10"–5' **Spread:** 18–36" **Flower color:** pink, rose, violet, white

IT'S REASSURING TO KNOW THERE
are different varieties of these popular plants—the way they revert
to the parent color when
they self-seed, you might
assume there is only one.
You can minimize the
self-seeding prob-
lem by removing
the spent flowers
and stems. There are
usually many stems, and
the plants get unwieldy if
you pinch them to encourage
branching. Let the plants grow
straight up and remove the flower
cluster and stem when the blooms
fade. If deadheading is not part of
your game plan, then just enjoy
the plant's natural growth cycle. New
blooms form at the peak of the plant as
the fading flowers beneath develop the
wonderful pods that contain so many
black seeds. Spider flowers are fabulous
plants, but usually they want to grow
only in my tomato patch, a space
strictly reserved for its namesake.

Planting

Seeding: Indoors in late winter; direct sow in spring. Chill seeds overnight before planting.

Planting out: After last frost

Spacing: 18–30"

Growing

Spider flowers prefer **full sun** but tolerate partial shade. Any kind of soil will do fine. Mix in plenty of **organic matter** to help the soil retain moisture. These plants are drought tolerant but look and perform better if watered regularly. Don't water excessively or they will become leggy.

Deadhead to prolong the blooming period and to minimize these plants' prolific self-sowing. Self-sowed seedlings will start coming up almost as soon as the seeds hit the ground and can become invasive. Fortunately, the new plants are very distinctive and can be spotted poking up where they don't belong, making them easy to pull up while they are still young. Flowers of self-sowed seedlings will most likely revert to light purple, the original species' color.

Tips

Spider flowers can be planted in groups at the back of a border. These plants are also effective in the center of an island bed. Use lower-growing plants around the edges to hide the leafless lower stems of the spider flower.

Try adding the seedpods to dried arrangements.

The flowers can be cut for fresh arrangements, although the plants have an unusual smell that is very noticeable up close.

C. hassleriana 'Helen Campbell'

Be careful when handling these plants because they have nasty barbs along the stems.

Recommended

C. hassleriana is a tall, upright plant with strong, supple, thorny stems. It grows up to 5' tall. The foliage and flowers of this plant have a strong, but not unpleasant, scent. **'Helen Campbell'** has white flowers. **Royal Queen Series** has flowers in all colors, available by individual color or as a mixture of all available colors. The varieties are named by their color; e.g., 'Cherry Queen,' 'Rose Queen' and 'Violet Queen.' Plants in this series resist fading. **'Sparkler Blush'** is a smaller plant than the species, to 36" tall. It bears pink flowers that fade to white. This cultivar was an All-America Selections winner for 2002.

C. hassleriana with *Nicotiana*, *Pelargonium* & *Impatiens* (above), *C. hassleriana* (below)

C. **'Linde Armstrong'** is a compact, thornless variety, growing 10–18" tall and bearing rosy pink blooms most of the summer. It is very heat tolerant and well suited to container growing.

C. serrulata (Rocky Mountain bee plant) is native to western North America. It is rarely available commercially, but the dwarf cultivar **'Solo'** can be purchased and grown from seed. 'Solo' grows 12–18" tall and bears 2–3", pink and white blooms. This plant is thornless.

Problems & Pests

Aphids may be a problem.

C. hassleriana 'Sparkler Blush'

'Hummingbird flower' might be a more appropriate name for these plants. They bloom through to fall, providing nectar for the tiny birds after many other flowers have finished blooming.

C. hassleriana

Statice

Limonium

Height: 12–24" **Spread:** 6–12" **Flower color:** blue, purple, pink, white, yellow, red, orange

THIS EVERLASTING IS OFTEN GROWN COMMERCIALLY FOR THE cut-flower trade, but more than enough varieties are available for gardeners to bypass the florist shop for a trip to the mixed border. Statice in the garden may look scruffy to flower purists, but it is a staple in bouquets either fresh or dried.

Also known as sea lavender, statice is native to the Mediterranean and is adapted to dry, saline habitats.

Planting

Seeding: Indoors in mid-winter; direct sow in spring

Planting out: After last frost

Spacing: 6–12"

Growing

Statice prefers **full sun.** The soil should be of **poor or average fertility, light, sandy** and **well drained.** This plant doesn't like having its roots disturbed, so if starting it indoors, use peat pots. Germination takes 14–21 days.

Tips

Statice makes an interesting addition to any sunny border, particularly in informal gardens. It is a perennial grown as an annual.

The basal leaves of statice form a rosette, and the flower stalks are sent up from the middle of the plant. Space the plants quite close together to make up for this lack of width.

Cut statice for drying late in summer, before the white center has come out on the bloom. Stand the stalks in a vase with about 1" of water and they will dry quite nicely on their own as the water is used up. If it's more convenient to keep them out of the way, you can hang them upside down in a cool, dry place.

Recommended

L. sinuatum forms a basal rosette of hairy leaves. Ridged stems bear clusters of small, papery flowers in blue, purple, pink or white. **'Fortress'** has strongly branching plants and flowers in several bright and pastel shades. The plants grow up to 24"

L. sinuatum

Statice can make an appealing temporary hedge in dry areas of the garden where color is often lacking.

tall. **Petite Bouquet Series** includes compact, 12" plants with flowers in blue, purple, pink, white and yellow. **'Sunset'** grows 24" tall and bears flowers in warm red, orange, peach, yellow, apricot and salmon shades.

Problems & Pests

Most problems can be avoided by providing a well-drained site and ensuring that there is good air circulation around the plants.

Stock

Matthiola

Height: 8–36" **Spread:** 12" **Flower color:** pink, purple, red, rose, white

ADD SOME SPICE TO YOUR GARDEN WITH STOCK. THESE PLANTS have long been esteemed for their fragrance, but they could stand a jazzier common name. Double-flowered varieties are often judged to be prettier than those with single flowers, and some low-growing varieties allow you to place the wonderful, spicy aroma in an edging situation or container.

When cutting stock flowers for arrangements, cut and then crush the ends of the woody stems so they will draw water more easily.

Planting

Seeding: Indoors in mid-winter or direct sow around last-frost date. Do not cover seeds because they require light to germinate.

Planting out: After last frost

Spacing: 12"

Growing

Stock plants prefer **full sun** but tolerate partial shade. The soil should be of **average fertility,** have lots of **organic matter** worked in and be **moist** but **well drained.**

M. incana Cinderella Series (above), *M. incana* (below)

Tips

Stocks can be used in mixed beds or in mass plantings.

Night-scented stock should be planted where its wonderful scent can be enjoyed in the evening—near windows that are left open, beside patios or along pathways. It is best to group night-scented stock with other plants because it tends to look wilted and bedraggled during the day but revives impressively at night.

Recommended

M. incana (stock) is the parent of many cultivar groups, with new ones introduced each year. Flower colors range from pink and purple to red, rose or white. The height can be 8–36", depending on the cultivar. **Cinderella Series** is popular. The compact plants in this series grow about 10" tall and have fragrant flowers in a variety of colors.

M. longipetala subsp. *bicornis* (night-scented stock, evening-scented stock) has pink or purple flowers that fill the evening air with

their scent. The plants grow 12–18" tall. **'Starlight Scentsation'** bears very fragrant flowers in a wide range of colors.

Problems & Pests

Root rot or other fungal problems may occur. Slugs may be attracted to the young foliage.

Strawflower
Everlasting
Xerochrysum (Bracteantha, Helichrysum)

Height: 6"–5' **Spread:** 9–24" **Flower color:** yellow, red, bronze, orange, pink, white, purple

THE TEXTURE OF STRAWFLOWER BLOSSOMS IS SO DIFFERENT FROM the soft, fragile petals of most blooms that it is almost disturbing the first time you examine them. Those papery extremities are really bracts (modified leaves) surrounding the tiny flowers, which are most often not noticed. Strawflower blooms nonstop, and its upright growth habit looks great in containers and mixed borders. Consider combining it with statice, cockscomb and the perennial yarrow *(Achillea)* for a dried-flower cutting garden.

Planting

Seeding: Indoors in early spring, or direct sow after last frost. Do not cover seeds; they require light to germinate.

Planting out: After last frost

Spacing: 9–18"

Growing

Strawflower prefers locations that receive **full sun**. The soil should be of **average fertility, neutral to alkaline, sandy, moist** and **well drained**. Strawflower is drought tolerant.

Be careful not to overwater, which causes the leaves to turn yellow and encourages disease.

Tips

Include strawflower in mixed beds, borders and containers. The lowest-growing varieties make good edging plants. Taller varieties may require staking.

The most popular use of strawflower is for fresh or dried arrangements. Harvest half-open blossoms; they will open fully as they dry.

X. bracteatum cultivars (photos this page)

Recommended

X. bracteatum (B. bracteata, H. bracteatum) is a tall, upright plant with gray-green foliage and brightly colored, papery flowers. The species can grow up to 5' tall, but cultivars are generally a bit more compact. **'Basket Bon Bon'** from Simply Beautiful grows 6–8" tall and 10" wide, with golden yellow blooms. **Chico Series** includes small, bushy plants reaching 12–15" in height and 9–12" in spread. Plants in this series bloom earlier than most strawflowers in a range of colors. **Dreamtime Series** plants grow 12" tall and 10" wide. They feature semi-double, yellow-centered flowers in shades of cream, yellow, orange and pink. *X. b. monstrosum* King Size Series produce large, double flowers 2–3" across, in bright shades of pink,

red, yellow, silvery white, orange, salmon, rose and white. The flowers are borne on 36" tall stems and work particularly well as dried flowers. **Sundaze Series** from Proven Winners grow 10–14" tall. The series includes 'Bronze Orange,' 'Golden Yellow,' 'Lemon Yellow,' 'Pink' and 'White.'

Problems & Pests

Strawflower is susceptible to downy mildew.

Sunflower

Helianthus

Height: dwarf varieties 24–36"; giants up to 15' **Spread:** 12–24"
Flower color: most commonly yellow but also orange, red, brown,
cream or bicolored; typically with brown, purple or rusty red centers

IF YOU HAVE FOLLOWED GARDENING AT ALL OVER THE LAST
decade, you'll be aware of the amazing transformation of sunflowers—from
the tallest plants in the garden to traffic-stopping smaller specimens. These
new varieties are far more adaptable to
the garden. It may have been cool to
grow a 10' stalk with a 24" flower
up there somewhere, but by
then I certainly would not call
it a decorative plant. Seek
out the new sunflowers,
available with the trademark
sunny yellow, bronze-
centered flowers as well as
many other colors and types of
blossoms.

*Plant a row of sunflowers at the
back of the vegetable garden, or
use one of the lower varieties
against a split-rail fence.*

Planting

Seeding: Indoors in late winter; direct sow in spring

Planting out: After last frost

Spacing: 12–24"

Growing

Sunflower grows best in **full sun**. The soil should be of **average fertility, humus rich, moist** and **well drained**.

The annual sunflower is an excellent plant for children to grow. The seeds are big and easy to handle, and they germinate quickly. The plants grow steadily upwards, and their progress can be measured until the flower finally appears on top of the tall plant. If planted along the wall of a two-story house, beneath an upstairs window, the progress can be observed from above as well as below, and the flowers will be easier to see.

'Teddy Bear' (above)

Tips

Use the lower-growing sunflower varieties in beds and borders. The tall varieties are effective at the backs of borders and make good screens and temporary hedges. The tallest varieties may need staking.

Birds will flock to the ripening seed-heads of your sunflowers, quickly plucking out the tightly packed seeds. If you plan to keep the seeds to eat, you may need to place a mesh net, the sort used to keep birds out of cherry trees, around the flower-heads until the seeds ripen. The net can be a bit of a nuisance and does not look too nice; most gardeners leave the flowers to the birds and buy seeds for eating.

Recommended

H. annuus (common sunflower) is often considered weedy, but the development of many new cultivars

has revived the use of this plant. '**Music Box**' is a branching plant that grows about 30" tall and has flowers in all colors, including some bicolors. '**Prado Red**' bears deep mahogany flowers and grows up to 5'. '**Russian Giant**' grows up to 10' tall and bears yellow flowers that develop large seeds. '**Teddy Bear**' has rather fuzzy-looking double flowers on compact plants 24–36" tall. '**Valentine**' bears creamy yellow flowers and grows up to 5'. '**Velvet Queen**' is a branching cultivar that bears many crimson red flowers.

Problems & Pests

Powdery mildew may affect these plants.

H. annuus *is grown as a crop for its seeds, which are used for roasting, snacking, baking, or producing oil or flour.*

Swan River Daisy

Brachyscome (Brachycome)

Height: 6–18"   **Spread:** equal to or slightly greater than height
Flower color: blue, pink, white, purple; usually with yellow centers

WHERE'S THE SWAN RIVER? IT'S IN SOUTHWESTERN AUSTRALIA, the native range of this plant. In American gardens, Swan River daisy has the reputation of being fussy but has been improved through breeding in the last decade. If you have heavy soil, consider using containers for this lacy, sweetly fragrant annual.

Planting

Seeding: Indoors in late winter; direct sow in mid-spring

Planting out: Early spring

Spacing: 12"

Growing

Swan River daisy prefers **full sun** but benefits from light shade in the afternoon. The soil should be **fertile** and **well drained**. Allow the soil to dry between waterings.

Plant out early because cool spring weather encourages compact, sturdy growth. This plant is frost tolerant and tends to die back when the summer gets too hot. Cut it back if it begins to fade, and don't plant it in hot areas of the garden.

B. iberidifolia (photos this page)

Tips

This versatile plant edges beds nicely and works well in rock gardens, mixed containers, hanging baskets and fresh arrangements.

Combine Swan River daisy with plants that mature later in the season. As Swan River daisy fades in July, its companions will be filling in and beginning to flower.

Recommended

B. **hybrids** are all heat-tolerant selections. **'Compact Pink'** grows 9–12" tall with dense, lacy foliage and light pink flowers. **'Hot Candy'** grows 6–10" tall and has larger leaves than other Swan River daisies. The flowers are bright pink. **'Toucan Tango'** grows 6–12" tall, with an equal spread. Its bright lavender to violet blue flowers bloom from late spring to fall.

B. iberidifolia forms a bushy, spreading, 18" mound of feathery foliage. Blue-purple or pink-purple, daisy-like flowers are borne all summer. Plants in the **Bravo Series** grow 8–10" tall. They bear flowers in white, blue, purple or pink and bloom profusely in a cool but bright spot in the garden. **Splendor Series** has dark-centered flowers in pink, purple or white on plants 9–12" tall.

Problems & Pests

Aphids, slugs and snails cause occasional trouble for this plant.

Sweet Alyssum
Alyssum
Lobularia

Height: 3–12" **Spread:** 6–24" **Flower color:** pink, purple, yellow, salmon, white, bicolored

FOR YEARS, SWEET ALYSSUM HAS PROVIDED LITERALLY MILES OF edging in Illinois, and it will most likely continue to serve that important purpose. Pinky rose varieties are more decorative if they work with your color scheme. White varieties self-seed prolifically and allow you to bypass replanting the following spring. If you've been disappointed with the late-summer performance of sweet alyssum, join the crowd—heat tolerance is not its strong suit. Shear back flagging plants to encourage a flush of fall flowers.

Planting

Seeding: Indoors in late winter; direct sow in spring

Planting out: Once soil has warmed

Spacing: 8–12"

Growing

Sweet alyssum prefers **full sun** but tolerates light shade. **Well-drained** soil of **average fertility** is preferred, but poor soil is tolerated. This plant dislikes having its roots disturbed, so if starting it indoors, use peat pots or pellets. Trim sweet alyssum back occasionally over the summer to keep it flowering and looking good.

Leave sweet alyssum plants out all winter. In spring, remove the previous year's growth to expose self-sowed seedlings below.

Tips

Sweet alyssum will creep around rock gardens, on rock walls and along the edges of beds. It is an excellent choice for seeding into cracks and crevices of walkway and patio stones, and once established it readily reseeds. It is also good for filling in spaces between taller plants in borders and in mixed containers.

'Pastel Carpet'

Recommended

L. maritima forms a low, spreading mound of foliage. The entire plant appears to be covered in tiny blossoms when it is in full flower. **'Pastel Carpet'** bears flowers in rose, white, violet and mauve. **'Snow Crystal'** bears large, bright white flowers profusely all summer. **Wonderland Series** offers a mix of all colors on compact plants.

Problems & Pests

Sweet alyssum rarely has problems but is sometimes afflicted with downy mildew.

Sweet Pea

Lathyrus

Height: 1–6' **Spread:** 6–12" **Flower color:** pink, red, purple, blue, salmon, pale yellow, peach, white, bicolored

A VINE WITH COLORFUL FLOWERS THAT SMELL WONDERFUL, TOO: who could ask for anything more? Grow sweet pea as early as you can get the seeds in the ground, because the plants will start to stall and die off as the temperatures rise. Provide a shading mulch to keep the roots cool. Sweet pea can make a dramatic fence or wall of color, given the right support, and there are nonclimbing forms as well. Just don't eat the seedpods—they're poisonous.

Sweet pea blossoms make attractive, long-lasting cut flowers. Cutting the flowers encourages still more blooms.

Planting

Seeding: Direct sow in early spring

Spacing: 6–12"

Growing

Sweet pea prefers **full sun** but tolerates light shade. The soil should be **fertile,** high in **organic matter, moist** and **well drained.** Fertilize very lightly with a low-nitrogen fertilizer during the flowering season. This plant will tolerate light frost. Deadhead all spent blooms.

Soak seeds in water for 24 hours or nick them with a nail file before planting them. Planting a second crop of sweet pea about a month after the first one will ensure a longer blooming period.

Tips

Sweet pea will grow up poles, trellises and fences or over rocks. The low-growing varieties form low, shrubby mounds.

To help prevent diseases from afflicting your sweet pea plants, avoid planting in the same location two years in a row.

Recommended

L. odoratus is the parent of many cultivars. **Bijou Series** is a popular heat-resistant variety that grows 18" tall, with an equal spread. It needs no support structure to grow upon. **'Bouquet Mix'** is a tall, climbing variety. **Supersnoop Series** is a sturdy bush type that needs no support. The flowers are fragrant. Pinch the tips of its long stems to encourage low growth.

Problems & Pests

Slugs and snails may eat the foliage of young plants. Root rot, mildew, rust and leaf spot may also afflict sweet pea occasionally.

Sweet William

Dianthus

Height: 6–30" **Spread:** 8–12" **Flower color:** white, pink, red, purple

THE ANNUAL VERSIONS OF *DIANTHUS* BLOOM IN EARLY SPRING, so they are candidates for fall planting alongside pansies—or look for them in garden centers as early in the season as possible. While most sweet williams are tall plants, much breeding has been done to draw down the height and lengthen flowering time. Fragrance is often an added bonus.

There are more than 300 annual and perennial species in the genus Dianthus.

Planting

Seeding: Direct sow *D. chinensis* in fall or indoors in spring; direct sow other sweet williams in late spring to early summer for bloom the following year

Planting out: Spring

Spacing: 6–12"

Growing

Sweet williams prefer **full sun** but tolerate some light shade. Keep these plants **sheltered** from strong winds and the hottest afternoon sun. A **light, neutral or alkaline, humus-rich, well-drained** soil is preferred. The most important factor in the successful cultivation of sweet williams is drainage. Mix gravel into their area of the flowerbed to encourage good drainage. Growing these plants in slightly alkaline soil will produce excellent color over a long period.

D. chinensis cultivars (above), 'Telstar Pink' (below)

The genus name, Dianthus, *is a combination of* Dios *(a form of the name Zeus) and* anthos, *'flower,' so it means 'flower of the gods.'*

'Corona Cherry Magic' (above),
D. barbatus cultivars (below)

Hanging baskets containing sweet williams will do best if fed with liquid fertilizer twice a month.

Deadhead as the flowers fade to prolong blooming. Leave a few flowers in place to go to seed, and the plants will self-seed quite easily. Seedlings may differ from the parent plants, often with new and interesting results.

Tips

Sweet williams are great for mass planting and for edging flower borders and walkways. Use these plants in the rock garden, or try them as cut flowers.

Recommended

D. barbatus (sweet william) is a biennial mostly grown as an annual. It reaches a height of 18–24" and spreads 8–12". Flattened clusters of often two-toned white, pink, red or purple-red flowers bloom in late spring to early summer. **'Hollandia Mix'** grows to 30". **'Indian Summer'** is a compact plant 6–8" tall. Plants in

the **Roundabout Series** grow 8–12"
tall and produce solid or two-toned
blooms in the first year from seed.
'**Summer Beauty**' reaches a height
of 12".

D. chinensis (china pink, annual
pink) is an erect, mound-forming
plant 6–30" tall and 8–12" wide. The
fragrant flowers come in pink, red,
white and light purple and are produced for an extended period in late
spring and summer. Many cultivars
are available. **Telstar Series** are
hybrids of *D. chinensis* and *D. barbatus,* usually listed under *D. chinensis.*
These plants grow 8–12" tall and
wide and produce blooms in shades
of pink, red and white in solid and
two-toned forms.

D. '**Corona Cherry Magic**' grows
8–10" tall and wide and has $2^1/_2$–3"
wide flowers that may be solid
cherry red or lavender, or bicolored.
This cultivar is a 2003 All-America
Selections winner.

D. '**Rainbow Loveliness**' grows to
24" tall and bears very fragrant flowers in shades of white, pink and
lavender.

Problems & Pests

Rust and *Fusarium* wilt may be
problems. Providing good drainage
and air circulation will keep most
fungal problems away. Occasional
problems with slugs and snails are
possible.

*The tiny, delicate petals of these
plants can be used to decorate
cakes. Be sure to remove the white
part at the base of the petals before
using them or they will be bitter.*

'Telstar Crimson'

Verbena
Garden Verbena
Verbena

Height: 4"–5' **Spread:** 10–36" **Flower color:** red, pink, purple, blue, yellow, scarlet, salmon, magenta, silver, peach or white; usually with white centers

VERBENAS MEET ALMOST EVERY CRITERION A GARDENER CAN demand of a plant. They fit many situations in the garden, come in a wide array of habits and color combinations, and grow reliably. New varieties come on the market annually, so choices abound. If you haven't grown 'Imagination,' give it a try—it is a wide-ranging plant in the ground and spectacular in a hanging basket.

If your plants become leggy or overgrown, cut them back by one-half to tidy them and promote lots of fall blooms.

Planting

Seeding: Indoors in mid-winter

Planting out: After last frost

Spacing: 10–18"

Growing

Verbenas grow best in **full sun**. The soil should be **fertile** and very **well drained**. Pinch back young plants for bushy growth.

Chill seeds one week before sowing. Moisten the soil before sowing seeds. Do not cover the seeds with soil. Place the entire seed tray or pot in darkness, and water only if the soil becomes very dry. Once the seeds germinate, move them into the light.

Tips

Use verbenas on rock walls and in beds, borders, rock gardens, containers, hanging baskets and window boxes. They make good substitutes for ivy-leaved geranium where the sun is hot and where a roof overhang keeps the mildew-prone verbenas dry.

V. x *hybrida* Tapien Series (above), other *V.* x *hybrida* cultivars (below)

The Romans, it is said, believed verbena could rekindle the flames of dying love. They named it Herba Veneris, *'plant of Venus.'*

V. bonariensis (above), *V. canadensis* (below)

Recommended

V. bonariensis forms a low clump of foliage from which tall, stiff, flower-bearing stems emerge. The small purple flowers are held in clusters. This plant grows up to 5' tall but spreads only 18–24". It may survive a mild winter, and it will self-seed. Butterflies love this plant.

V. canadensis (clump verbena, rose vervain) is a low-growing, spreading plant native to south-central and southeastern North America. It grows up to 18" tall and spreads up to 36". Clusters of pink flowers appear from mid-summer to fall. It may survive a mild winter. Plants in the **Babylon Series** grow to 7" tall, resist mildew and flower early. This series produces abundant flowers in shades of pink, purple and red. 'Homestead Purple' is the most common cultivar; it is more common than the species in gardens. It bears dark purple flowers all summer and resists mildew. **Tukana Series** plants also grow to 7" tall and produce flowers in shades of blue, salmon, scarlet and white.

V. x hybrida is a bushy plant that may be upright or spreading. It bears clusters of small flowers in shades of white, purple, blue, pink, red or yellow. **Aztec Series** from Simply Beautiful includes plants 16–18" tall and 10–12" wide. They feature flowers in an impressive array of purples, pinks, reds and white. '**Imagination**' (*V. x speciosa* 'Imagination') is a spreading plant that grows 12–24" tall and 24–36" wide. This All-America Selections winner produces clusters of intense violet blue flowers. **'Peaches and Cream'** is a spreading plant with flowers that open a soft peach color and fade to white. **Romance Series** has red, pink, purple or white flowers, with white eyes. The plants grow up to 8–10" tall. **'Showtime'** bears brightly colored flowers on compact plants that grow up to 10" tall and spread 18". **Tapien Series** plants from Proven Winners grow 4–6" tall and 10–18" wide. These low-growing, well-branched plants flower in white and shades of pink and purple. **Temari Series** plants resist mildew, tolerate heat and have vigorous, spreading growth. The flowers come in a range of colors on plants 8–14" tall.

V. x *hybrida* cultivar (above), *V. bonariensis* (below)

V. pendula **Superbena Series** from Proven Winners includes vigorous, upright to trailing plants 6–12" tall and 10–14" wide. The plants have excellent mildew resistance and boast large flowers in intense shades of red, pink and purple.

Problems & Pests

Aphids, whiteflies, slugs and snails may be troublesome. Avoid fungal problems by making sure there is good air circulation around verbena plants.

'Homestead Purple' was discovered by horticulturalists Allan Armitage and Michael Dirr as a chance hybrid on a Georgia homestead.

Vinca
Madagascar Periwinkle, Vinca Rosea
Catharanthus

Height: 10–24" **Spread:** equal to or greater than height **Flower color:** red, rose, pink, mauve, apricot or white, often with contrasting centers

WITH THEIR CHEERFUL FLOWERS AND AMAZING HEAT TOLERANCE, vincas have been heavily promoted by the garden industry. The flower petals are often lined with darker colors, extending from a darker eye in the center. The adaptability of this plant and its cultivars makes them surefire winners. One of the best annuals to use in front of homes on busy streets, vinca will bloom happily despite exposure to exhaust fumes and dust.

Planting

Seeding: Indoors in mid-winter

Planting out: After last frost

Spacing: 8–18"

Growing

Vinca prefers **full sun** but tolerates partial shade. Any **well-drained** soil is fine. This plant tolerates pollution and drought, but it prefers to be watered regularly. It doesn't like to be too wet or too cold. Plant vinca after the soil has warmed.

Keep seedlings warm and take care not to overwater them. The soil temperature should be 55°–64° F for seeds to germinate.

Tips

Vinca will do well in the sunniest, warmest part of the garden. Plant it in a bed along an exposed driveway or against the south-facing wall of the house. It can also be used in hanging baskets, in planters and as a temporary groundcover.

This plant is a perennial that is grown as an annual. In a bright room, it can be grown as a house-plant.

Recommended

C. roseus (*Vinca rosea*) forms a 12–24" mound of strong stems. The flowers are pink, red or white, often with contrasting centers. '**Apricot Delight**' is a 10–12" plant that bears pale apricot flowers with bright raspberry red centers. **Cooler Series** plants are 10–14" tall. They bear light-colored flowers with darker, contrasting centers. All-America Selections winner '**Jaio Dark Red**' is

'Jaio Scarlet Eye' (above), *C. roseus* (below)

a 10–15" plant that has large ($2^{1}/_{2}$" wide), very red flowers with a small white eye. '**Jaio Scarlet Eye**,' another AAS winner, produces a profusion of bright, rosy red flowers with a small white eye. It grows to 12" tall. Plants in the **Pacifica Series** have flowers in various colors on compact plants 12" tall.

Problems & Pests

Slugs can be troublesome. Most rot and other fungal problems can be avoided by not overwatering.

Viola
Pansy, Johnny-Jump-Up
Viola

Height: 3–10" **Spread:** 4–12" **Flower color:** blue, purple, red, orange, yellow, pink, white, multi-colored

IT'S A BIT HARD TO BELIEVE JOHNNY-JUMP-UPS AND PANSIES ARE such close botanical relatives, since they are so different in size. Johnny-jump-ups are the size of perennial violets, but their dainty flowers are multi-hued. Pansies are, well, pansies. All prefer cool temperatures. It has taken many years to persuade consumers to consider planting pansies in fall, so that they can be enjoyed again the following spring. In warmer areas of the state, some pansies bloom right through a mild winter.

These versatile plants are perfect for planting early in the season, when frost still threatens.

Planting

Seeding: Indoors in early winter or mid-summer

Planting out: Early spring or early fall

Spacing: 6"

Growing

Violas prefer **full sun** but tolerate partial shade. The soil should be **fertile, moist** and **well drained**.

Violas do best when the weather is cool. They may die back completely in summer. Plants may rejuvenate in fall, but it is often easier to plant new ones in fall and not take up summer garden space with annuals that don't look their best.

Direct sowing is not recommended. Sow seeds indoors in early winter for spring flowers and in mid-summer for fall and early-winter blooms. More seeds will germinate if they are kept in darkness until they sprout. Place seed trays in a dark closet or cover with dark plastic or layers of newspaper to block out the light.

Tips

Violas can be used in beds and borders, and they are popular for mixing in with spring-flowering bulbs. They can also be grown in containers. The large-flowered pansies are preferred for early-spring color among primroses in garden beds.

Recommended

V. tricolor (Johnny-jump-up) is a popular species. It grows 3–6" tall and 4–6" wide. The flowers are purple, white and yellow, usually in combination, although several varieties have

V. x *wittrockiana* cultivar (above), 'Ultima Morpho' (below)

V. tricolor

flowers in a single color, frequently purple. This plant thrives in gravel. **'Bowles Black'** has dark purple flowers that appear almost black. The center of each flower is yellow. **'Helen Mound'** ('Helen Mount') bears large flowers in the traditional, cheerful purple, yellow and white combination.

V. x *wittrockiana* (pansy) plants grow 8–10" tall and 6–12" wide. The flowers come in blue, purple, red, orange, yellow, pink or white, often multi-colored or with face-like markings. **'Floral Dance'** is popular for spring and fall displays as it is quite cold hardy; it has flowers in a variety of solid colors and multi-colors. **Imperial Series** bears large flowers in a range of unique colors. For example, 'Imperial Frosty Rose' has flowers with deep rose pink centers that gradually pale to

Perfume bottles with narrow necks make wonderful small vases for displaying the cut flowers of violas. The more you pick, the more profusely the plants will bloom. These flowers are also among the easiest to press between sheets of wax paper, weighted down with stacks of books.

white near the edges of the petals. **Joker Series** has bicolored or multi-colored flowers with distinctive face-like markings. The flowers come in all colors. '**Maxim Marina**' bears light blue flowers with white-rimmed, dark blue blotches at the center. This cultivar tolerates both high and low temperatures. '**Ultima Morpho**' is a unique bicolor. Among its variations are azure to mid-blue upper petals over bright lemon yellow lower petals. It is a 2002 All-America Selections winner. **Watercolor Series** is a newer group of cultivars with flowers in delicate pastel shades.

Problems & Pests

Slugs and snails can be problems. Fungal diseases can be avoided through good air circulation and good drainage.

V. x *wittrockiana* cultivars (above) & with tulips (below)

Viola flowers are edible and make delightful garnishes on salads and desserts. Make candied violets by brushing the flowers with whipped egg white and sprinkling them with superfine sugar. Allow them to dry overnight.

Wishbone Flower

Torenia

Height: 6–12" **Spread:** 6–12" **Flower color:** purple, pink, blue, burgundy, white; often bicolored with a yellow spot on the lower petal

FIND THE 'WISHBONE' BY GENTLY PULLING APART THE OUTER petals of these flowers to find a joined pair of stamens (male flower parts) that resemble the wishbone of a turkey. The snapdragon-like blooms form in clusters on compact plants, making wishbone flower ideal as a bedding plant or in containers. If potted before the first frost, it can be brought indoors to flower in a bright room.

Planting

Seeding: Indoors in late winter

Planting out: After last-frost date

Spacing: About 8"

Growing

Wishbone flower prefers **light shade** but tolerates partial and full shade. The soil should be **fertile, light, humus rich** and **moist**. This plant requires regular watering.

Don't cover the seeds when planting; they need light to germinate.

Tips

Wishbone flower can be massed in a shaded bed or border, used as an edging plant or added to a mixed container or hanging basket. It makes a nice change in shade gardens if you find yourself overusing impatiens. Try wishbone flower near a water feature, where the soil may remain moist for extended periods.

Recommended

T. fournieri is a bushy, rounded to upright plant. It grows up to 12" tall, with an equal or lesser spread. Its purple flowers have yellow throats. **Clown Series** features compact plants that grow 6–10" tall. The flowers may be purple, blue, pink or white. **Duchess Series** has compact plants, up to 6" tall, and bears larger flowers in a range of colors. **Summer Wave Series** are fast-growing, heat-loving plants. The series includes 'Amethyst,' with rich magenta purple flowers; 'Blue,' with violet-tinged blue flowers; and 'Large Violet,' with large, deep violet flowers.

Problems & Pests

Fungal problems can occur in overly wet soils. Moist but not soggy soils are ideal.

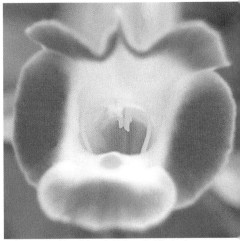

T. fournieri cultivar (above), *T. fournieri* (below)

Wishbone flower is one of the few annuals that tolerates constantly damp (but not waterlogged) soils.

Xeranthemum
Immortelle
Xeranthemum

Height: 24" **Spread:** 18" **Flower color:** white, purple, red or pink

---

LONG-LASTING BLOOMS ARE THE HIGHEST VIRTUE OF ANNUAL plants. And not only does xeranthemum last for many weeks in the garden, but its flowers also last a long time when harvested and dried. If you choose to make it an everlasting, cut the blooms before they are fully open. Hang the stems upside down in the same way you would plants of other species used for dried flowers.

Xeranthemum is only rarely troubled by pest and disease problems.

Planting

Seeding: Sow indoors in mid-spring or direct sow in mid- to late spring

Planting out: After the last frost

Spacing: 12–18"

Growing

Xeranthemum prefers **full sun** in a **sheltered** site. The soil should be **average to fertile** and **well drained**.

In windy or exposed locations, staking may be required. Insert twiggy branches into the soil around the young plants to provide support as they grow taller.

Tips

These flowers make an interesting addition to the middle of the border, but they are best known as cut flowers. Cut the blooms before they are completely open for fresh or dried arrangements.

Recommended

X. annuum is an upright plant with slender branched stems. It bears

The alternative common name immortelle refers to the long-lasting color of the blooms, even when dried.

single or semi-double, daisy-like, pink or sometimes white flowers. **'Flore Pleno'** bears double flowers in all colors. **'Lumina Double'** has double flowers in bright colors. **'Snow Lady'** ('Snowlady') features single white flowers.

Zinnia

Zinnia

Height: 6–36" **Spread:** 12" **Flower color:** red, yellow, gold, green, purple, orange, pink, white, maroon, brown

ZINNIAS ARE AMONG THOSE LOVE 'EM OR HATE 'EM FLOWERS. These staple garden plants provide lots of colorful flowers on sturdy stems, and they are nearly foolproof to grow, even thriving in a container you may sometimes forget to water. On the flip side, older varieties were so suscept-ible to powdery mildew that veteran gardeners developed a bias against all zinnias. As with so many annuals, breeding has brought improvements to this old standby. Try the Profusion Series; these compact bedding plants in several colors may help redefine how you think about zinnias.

Planting

Seeding: Indoors in late winter; direct sow after last frost

Planting out: After last frost

Spacing: 6–12"

Growing

Zinnias grow best in **full sun**. The soil should be **fertile,** rich in **organic matter, moist** and **well drained.** When starting seeds indoors, plant them in individual peat pots to avoid disturbing the roots when transplanting.

Deadhead zinnias to keep them flowering and looking their best. To keep mildew from the leaves, plant mildew-resistant varieties and avoid wetting the foliage when you water.

Tips

Zinnias are useful in beds, borders, containers and cutting gardens. The

Though zinnias are quite drought tolerant, they will grow best if watered thoroughly when the soil dries out. Use a soaker hose to avoid wetting the leaves.

'Profusion White'

Z. haageana cultivar

The name Zinnia *honors Johann Gottfried Zinn (1727–59), the German botany professor who first grew one of the South American zinnias from seed.*

Z. elegans 'California Giants'

dwarf varieties can be used as edging plants. These plants often bloom right up to the first frost and are wonderful for fall color. Combine the rounded zinnia flowers with the spiky blooms of sun-loving salvia, or use the taller varieties in front of sunflowers.

Recommended

Z. elegans flowers come in several forms, including single, double and cactus-flowered. On a cactus-flowered bloom, the petals appear to be rolled into tubes like the spines of a cactus. **'California Giants'** are bushy plants growing to 36" and bearing large double flowers in a wide range of colors. **'Peter Pan'** grows up to 12" tall, but it starts blooming early at 6", with flowers in mixed colors. **Thumbelina Series** has small flowers in all colors on dwarf, 6", weather-resistant plants.

Z. haageana (*Z. angustifolia;* Mexican zinnia) is a bushy plant with narrow leaves. It grows 6–24" tall, spreads 12" and bears bright orange, daisy-like flowers. This species tolerates heat and drought and resists pests. **'Crystal White'** bears white, daisy-like flowers on plants that grow 6–8" tall. It makes a wonderful edger for beds and borders. **'Persian Carpet'** bears bicolored and tricolored flowers in orange, red, yellow, gold, maroon and brown.

Zinnias make excellent, long-lasting cut flowers for fresh arrangements.

Z. **Profusion Series** are fast-growing, mildew-resistant, compact hybrids. These All-America Selections grow 10–18" tall and bear flowers in bright cherry red, orange or white.

Problems & Pests

Zinnias can be prone to mildew and other fungal problems. Prevent such problems by ensuring good air circulation and drainage for the plants, and by planting resistant varieties.

Z. elegans 'California Giants' (above)

OTHER ANNUALS TO CONSIDER

Chrysanthemum
Chrysanthemum carinatum

Upright plant with fleshy, finely divided foliage. Grows about 24" tall and spreads 12". Sometimes called painted daisy, referring to the contrasting multi-colored bands on petal bases. Both the Court Jesters Mixed and Rainbow Series cultivars have red, white, yellow and purple multi-colored, daisy-like flowers. Grow in **full sun** or **partial shade** with **average, well-drained** soil. Deadhead to prolong blooming. Several successive sowings will keep the colorful show going all summer. Useful and attractive in informal beds, borders and planters; the blooms make good cut flowers. People with sensitive skin can develop contact dermatitis after touching some chrysanthemums.

Cathedral Bells
Cobaea scandens

Vigorous climbing vine, native to Mexico. Can climb and spread 6–25' or more. Fragrant pale green or creamy white, cup-shaped flowers darken to purple as they mature. Grow in **full sun** in a **sheltered** location with **average, moist, well-drained** soil. Too much nitrogen fertilizer encourages leafy growth but delays and reduces flowering. Provide a trellis, arbor or chain-link fence for plants to climb. Overwinter indoors, or take cuttings in late summer and root them to provide plants for the following summer.

Crocosmia
Crocosmia 'Lucifer'

Spreading plant 36" tall and about 15–18" wide, with long, strap-like leaves and bright red flowers on one-sided spikes. Blooms from mid-July through August. This tender perennial prefers **sheltered** spots in **full sun,** with **humus-rich, moist, well-drained** soil of **average fertility**. Grows from corms that can be dug up in fall and stored in slightly damp sawdust or peat moss in a cool, dark place over winter. Start seed indoors or out in early spring. Create a striking display by planting in masses with about 12" space between plants.

Toadflax
Linaria maroccana
& cultivars

Erect, wispy-looking
plants 6–24" tall and 6"
wide. Two-lipped flowers
bloom in summer.
Species' flowers are violet,
pink or white, with lower
lip marked in orange to
yellow. Cultivars flower
in solids and bicolors of
white, pink, purple,
orange, yellow or deep
red. Grow in **full sun**. Soil
should be **sandy,** of **low to
moderate fertility** and
well drained. Plants may
stall and die out in sum-
mer heat. Direct sow as
soon as ground thaws in
spring. Deadhead as
flower spikes fade because
plants self-seed easily.
Most effective planted in
masses. Good in the rock
garden or in an annual or
mixed border.

Pimpernel
Anagallis monellii

Erect, free-branching,
frost-tender perennial
9–18" tall and 9–16" wide.
Deep blue flowers bloom
for an extended period in
summer. Petals may be
tinged red on undersides.
Grow in **full sun** in **moist,
well-drained** soil of **average fertility;** does well in
sandy soils. Provides
strong blue color at the
front of the border or in
a rock garden; also excellent in containers. Start
seed indoors in spring or
outdoors in cold frame,
and plant out after last
frost. Cultivars from
Proven Winners are com-
pact and very free flowering, with blooms in blue
and a wonderful orange.

Mexican Mint
Plectranthus

Bushy plants 8–12" tall
and about 36" in spread.
Both *P. amionicus* and
P. forsteri are commonly
available. Grow in **light or
partial shade** with **fertile,
moist, well-drained** soil.
These trailing plants
make fabulous fillers for
hanging baskets and
mixed containers. Place
near a walkway or other
area where people will be
able to brush past the
plants and smell the
spicy-scented foliage.
Plants root easily from
cuttings; start some in
late summer to grow
indoors through winter.

HEIGHT LEGEND: Low: < 12" • Medium: 12–24" • Tall: > 24"

SPECIES
by Common Name

	COLOR									SOWING		HEIGHT		
	White	Pink	Red	Orange	Yellow	Blue	Purple	Green	Foliage	Indoors	Direct	Low	Medium	Tall
African Daisy	*	*		*	*		*			*			*	
Ageratum	*	*				*	*			*	*	*	*	*
Agrostemma	*	*					*			*	*			*
Amaranth			*		*			*	*	*	*			*
Angel's Trumpet	*				*		*			*			*	*
Angel Wings	*	*				*	*						*	
Baby's Breath	*	*					*			*	*		*	*
Bachelor's Buttons	*	*	*			*	*			*	*		*	*
Bacopa	*		*			*	*					*		
Begonia	*	*	*	*	*				*	*		*	*	
Bidens					*					*	*	*	*	
Black-eyed Susan			*	*	*					*	*	*	*	*
Black-eyed Susan Vine	*			*	*		*			*	*			*
Blanket Flower			*	*	*					*	*		*	*
Blood Flower			*	*	*					*				*
Blue Throatwort						*	*			*	*		*	*
Browallia	*					*	*			*		*	*	
Caladium									*				*	
Calendula				*	*					*	*	*	*	
Calibrachoa	*	*	*	*	*	*	*					*		
Canterbury Bells	*	*				*	*			*			*	*
Cockscomb		*	*	*	*		*			*	*	*	*	*
Coleus									*	*		*	*	*
Coreopsis			*	*	*					*	*	*	*	*
Cosmos	*	*	*	*	*		*			*	*		*	*
Creeping Zinnia				*	*						*	*		
Cup Flower	*					*	*			*		*		
Cuphea	*	*	*				*	*		*		*	*	

Hardy	Half-hardy	Tender	Sun	Part Shade	Light Shade	Shade	Moist	Well Drained	Dry	Fertile	Average	Poor	Page Number	SPECIES by Common Name
	*		*				*	*			*		50	African Daisy
		*	*				*	*		*			54	Ageratum
	*		*					*				*	58	Agrostemma
		*	*					*			*	*	60	Amaranth
		*	*				*	*		*			64	Angel's Trumpet
		*	*				*	*		*			68	Angel Wings
*			*	*				*				*	70	Baby's Breath
*			*	*			*	*		*			72	Bachelor's Buttons
		*		*			*	*			*		74	Bacopa
		*	*	*	*			*		*			76	Begonia
		*	*				*	*		*	*		82	Bidens
	*		*	*			*	*			*		84	Black-eyed Susan
		*	*	*	*		*	*		*			86	Black-eyed Susan Vine
*			*					*			*	*	88	Blanket Flower
		*	*					*			*	*	90	Blood Flower
		*	*	*			*	*			*		92	Blue Throatwort
		*	*	*	*	*		*		*			94	Browallia
		*		*	*	*	*	*		*			96	Caladium
*			*	*				*			*		100	Calendula
	*		*				*	*		*			102	Calibrachoa
*			*				*	*		*			104	Canterbury Bells
		*	*				*	*		*			106	Cockscomb
		*	*	*	*		*	*		*	*		110	Coleus
*			*					*		*	*		114	Coreopsis
		*	*					*			*	*	116	Cosmos
		*	*					*			*		120	Creeping Zinnia
	*		*	*			*	*			*		122	Cup Flower
		*	*	*				*			*		124	Cuphea

HEIGHT LEGEND: Low: < 12" • Medium: 12–24" • Tall: > 24"

SPECIES
by Common Name

	White	Pink	Red	Orange	Yellow	Blue	Purple	Green	Foliage	Indoors	Direct	Low	Medium	Tall
Dahlberg Daisy				*	*					*	*	*		
Dahlia	*	*	*	*	*		*			*	*	*	*	*
Diascia		*								*		*	*	
Dusty Miller									*	*			*	
Fan Flower						*	*			*		*		
Flowering Maple	*	*	*	*	*					*			*	*
Flowering Tobacco	*	*	*		*		*	*		*	*	*	*	*
Four O'Clock Flower	*	*	*		*		*			*	*		*	*
Fuchsia	*	*	*	*			*					*	*	*
Gazania	*	*	*	*	*					*	*	*		
Geranium	*	*	*	*			*			*		*	*	*
Globe Amaranth	*	*	*	*			*			*		*	*	*
Heliotrope	*					*	*			*		*	*	*
Hollyhock	*	*	*	*	*		*			*				*
Hyacinth Bean	*						*			*	*			*
Impatiens	*	*	*	*	*		*			*		*	*	*
Lantana	*	*	*	*	*		*						*	*
Larkspur	*	*				*	*			*	*		*	*
Lavatera	*	*	*				*			*	*		*	*
Licorice Plant									*			*	*	
Lobelia	*	*	*			*	*			*		*		
Love-in-a-Mist	*	*				*	*			*	*		*	
Marigold			*	*	*					*		*	*	*
Mexican Sunflower			*	*	*					*	*			*
Mignonette			*		*			*		*	*		*	
Monkey Flower		*	*	*	*					*		*		
Morning Glory	*	*	*	*	*	*	*			*	*			*
Musk Mallow		*	*	*	*					*	*		*	*

Hardy	Half-hardy	Tender	Sun	Part Shade	Light Shade	Shade	Moist	Well Drained	Dry	Fertile	Average	Poor	Page Number	SPECIES by Common Name
*			*					*			*	*	128	Dahlberg Daisy
		*	*				*	*		*			130	Dahlia
	*		*				*	*		*			134	Diascia
	*		*					*		*			138	Dusty Miller
		*	*		*		*	*		*			140	Fan Flower
		*	*	*			*	*		*			142	Flowering Maple
		*	*	*	*		*	*		*			146	Flowering Tobacco
		*	*					*	*				150	Four O'Clock Flower
		*		*	*		*	*		*			152	Fuchsia
		*	*					*			*	*	156	Gazania
		*	*					*	*				158	Geranium
		*	*					*			*		162	Globe Amaranth
		*	*				*	*		*			164	Heliotrope
*			*					*			*	*	168	Hollyhock
	*		*				*	*			*	*	170	Hyacinth Bean
		*		*			*	*		*			172	Impatiens
	*		*				*	*		*			176	Lantana
*			*		*		*	*		*			178	Larkspur
		*	*	*				*			*		180	Lavatera
	*		*					*			*	*	182	Licorice Plant
*			*	*			*	*		*			184	Lobelia
*			*					*			*		186	Love-in-a-Mist
	*	*	*					*			*		188	Marigold
		*	*					*			*	*	192	Mexican Sunflower
*			*	*				*			*		194	Mignonette
	*	*			*	*	*			*			196	Monkey Flower
		*	*					*			*	*	198	Morning Glory
		*	*					*		*			202	Musk Mallow

HEIGHT LEGEND: Low: < 12" • Medium: 12–24" • Tall: > 24"

SPECIES by Common Name	COLOR									SOWING		HEIGHT		
	White	Pink	Red	Orange	Yellow	Blue	Purple	Green	Foliage	Indoors	Direct	Low	Medium	Tall
Nasturtium	*	*	*	*	*					*	*		*	*
Nemesia	*	*	*	*	*	*	*			*		*	*	
Passion Flower	*	*				*								*
Persian Shield									*				*	*
Petunia	*	*	*		*	*	*			*		*	*	
Phlox	*	*	*		*	*	*				*	*	*	
Pincushion Flower	*	*	*			*	*			*	*		*	*
Polka Dot Plant									*	*			*	
Poppy	*	*	*	*	*		*				*		*	*
Portulaca	*	*	*	*	*		*			*		*		
Rose-of-Heaven		*									*	*	*	
Salvia	*	*	*	*	*	*	*			*	*		*	*
Snapdragon	*	*	*	*	*		*			*	*	*	*	*
Spider Flower	*	*					*			*	*		*	*
Statice	*	*	*	*	*	*	*			*	*		*	
Stock	*	*	*				*			*	*	*	*	*
Strawflower	*	*	*	*	*		*			*	*		*	*
Sunflower			*	*	*					*	*			*
Swan River Daisy	*	*				*	*			*	*	*	*	
Sweet Alyssum	*	*			*		*			*	*	*		
Sweet Pea	*	*	*		*	*	*				*		*	*
Sweet William	*	*	*				*			*	*	*	*	*
Verbena	*	*	*		*	*	*			*		*	*	*
Vinca	*	*	*				*			*			*	
Viola	*	*	*	*	*	*	*			*	*	*		
Wishbone Flower	*	*				*	*			*		*		
Xeranthemum	*	*	*				*				*			*
Zinnia	*	*	*	*	*		*	*		*	*	*	*	*

Hardy	Half-hardy	Tender	Sun	Part Shade	Light Shade	Shade	Moist	Well Drained	Dry	Fertile	Average	Poor	Page Number	SPECIES by Common Name
		*	*				*	*			*	*	204	Nasturtium
		*	*				*	*		*			208	Nemesia
*			*	*			*	*			*		210	Passion Flower
		*		*	*	*	*	*		*	*		212	Persian Shield
	*		*					*		*	*		214	Petunia
*			*				*	*		*			218	Phlox
	*		*				*	*		*	*		220	Pincushion Flower
		*	*				*	*			*		222	Polka Dot Plant
*			*					*		*	*		224	Poppy
		*	*					*				*	228	Portulaca
		*	*		*		*	*		*			230	Rose-of-Heaven
	*	*	*				*	*		*	*		232	Salvia
	*		*					*		*			236	Snapdragon
	*		*				*						240	Spider Flower
		*	*					*			*	*	244	Statice
*			*				*	*			*		246	Stock
	*		*				*	*			*		248	Strawflower
*			*				*	*			*		250	Sunflower
	*		*		*			*		*			254	Swan River Daisy
*			*					*			*		256	Sweet Alyssum
*			*				*	*		*			258	Sweet Pea
		*	*					*		*			260	Sweet William
*		*	*					*		*			264	Verbena
		*	*					*					268	Vinca
*			*				*	*		*			270	Viola
		*			*		*			*			274	Wishbone Flower
	*		*					*		*	*	*	276	Xeranthemum
		*	*				*	*		*			278	Zinnia

GLOSSARY

acid soil: soil with a pH lower than 7.0

alkaline soil: soil with a pH higher than 7.0

annual: a plant that germinates, flowers, sets seed and dies in one growing season

basal leaves: leaves that form from the crown, at the base of the plant

biennial: a plant that germinates and produces stems, roots and leaves in the first growing season; it flowers, sets seed and dies in the second growing season

crown: the part of a plant at or just below soil level where the shoots join the roots

cultivar: a *cultiv*ated plant *var*iety with one or more differences from the species, e.g., in flower or leaf color or disease resistance

deadhead: to remove spent flowers to maintain a neat appearance and encourage a longer blooming period

direct sow: to sow seeds directly in the garden soil where the plants are to grow, as opposed to sowing first in pots or flats and transplanting

dormancy: to remove some flowerbuds to improve the size or quality of the remaining ones

double flower: a flower with an unusually large number of petals, often caused by mutation of the stamens into petals

genus: a category of biological classification between the species and family levels; the first word in a scientific name indicates the genus, e.g., *Centaurea* in *Centaurea cyanus*

half-hardy: a plant able to survive the climatic conditions of a region if protected from heavy frost or cold

harden off: to gradually acclimatize plants that have been growing in a protective environment (usually indoors) to a more harsh environment (usually outdoors in spring)

hardy: able to survive unfavorable conditions, such as cold weather, without protection

humus: decomposed or decomposing organic material in the soil

hybrid: a plant resulting from natural or human-induced cross-breeding between varieties, species or genera; the hybrid expresses features of each parent plant

neutral soil: soil with a pH of 7.0

perennial: a plant that takes three or more years to complete its life cycle; a herbaceous

perennial normally dies back to the ground over winter and resprouts each spring

pH: a measure of acidity or alkalinity (the lower the pH, the higher the acidity); the pH of soil influences nutrient availability for plants

rootball: the root mass and surrounding soil of a container-grown plant or a plant dug out of the ground

self-cleaning: describes plants whose flowers drop after they finish blooming, eliminating the need for deadheading

self-seed (self-sow): to reproduce by means of seeds without human assistance, so that new plants constantly replace those that die

semi-double flower: a flower with petals that form two or three rings

sepal: segment of the outermost ring (calyx) of a typical flower; usually green and leaf-like, but sometimes large, colorful and petal-like

single flower: a flower with a single ring of typically four or five petals

species: the original plant from which cultivars and varieties are derived; the fundamental unit of biological classification, indicated by a two-part scientific name, e.g., *Centaurea cyanus* (*cyanus* is the specific epithet)

sport: an atypical plant or part of a plant that arises spontaneously through mutation; some sports are horticulturally desirable and propagated as new cultivars

subshrub: a plant that is somewhat shrubby or woody at the base; tender subshrubs may be grown as annuals

subspecies (subsp.): a naturally occurring, regional form of a species

tender: incapable of surviving the climatic conditions of a given region and requiring protection from frost or cold

true: describes the reliable passing of desired traits from a parent plant to seed-grown offspring; also called breeding true to type

tuber: a swollen part of a root or underground stem, modified for food storage; *Dahlia* plants, for example, have root tubers

variegated: describes foliage that is more than one color, often patched or striped or with differently colored leaf margins

variety (var.): a naturally occurring variant of a species; placed below the level of subspecies in biological classification

INDEX OF PLANT NAMES